THE
SEASONS

A Collection of Poetry and Prose on Spring,
Summer, Autumn and Winter

Compiled by Robin Barratt

With...

Akanksha Bhatnagar, Abigail George, Barbara E. Robinson, Beaton
Galafa, Bernadette Perez, Bill Cox, Brian Langley, Brigette Furlonger,
Chrys Salt, Clare Lightfoot, Clare Roslington, Courtney Speedy, David
Hollywood, David Watt, Don Adams, Farha A. Jaleel, Gabriella
Garofalo, Greg Bogaerts, Jasmine Kang, Jennifer Riggs, John Karl
Stokes, John R. Sabine, John Tunaley, Justin Fox, Dr. Kapardeli
Eftichia, Kathleen Bleakley, Kathleen Boyle, Kirsty A. Niven, LindaAnn
Lo Schiavo, Linda M. Crate, Lynette Cupido, Madhavi Tiwary, Mantz
Yorke, Mary Anne Zammit, Mary Coons, Mavis Atha, Olivia Matthews,
Pamela Scott, Rebecca Sutton, Rosemary Rigsby, Sara Madan,
S'busiso Manqa, Sourabh Acharya, Stella Carruthers, Terry Hickland
and Tracy Davidson.

Published by Robin Barratt
ISBN: 978-1546891161
© Robin Barratt 2017 and all the authors herein

W: www.collectionsofpoetryandprose.com
E: Editor@collectionsofpoetryandprose.com
E: RobinBarratt@yahoo.com

Committed to publishing the works and words of writers and poets around the world

Our Other Collections...

BETRAYAL
A Collection of Poetry and Prose on Betrayal and Being Betrayed

HAPPY
A Collection of Poetry and Prose on Happiness and Being Happy

WAR
A Collection of Poetry and Prose about the Bravery
and Horror of War

TRAVEL
A Collection of Poetry and Prose about Travels and Travelling

LOVE
A Collection of Poetry and Prose on Loving and Being in Love

LONELY
A Collection of Poetry and Prose on Loneliness and Being Alone

Contents By Title...

AUTUMN

WINTER

Contents By Author...

Introduction

By Robin Barratt

Welcome to *SEASONS - A Collection of Poetry and Prose on Spring, Summer, Autumn and Winter*, the seventh in our Collections of Poetry and Prose book series.

SEASONS is another varied and unique collection of poetry and short prose from both established and aspiring writers and poets around the world. There are so very many brilliant and brilliantly talented writers out there who never get their works seen or their words read, and so our objectives with this book series are to showcase poets and writers, and to offer them another platform to display their work. It doesn't matter where you live, your age, your culture or your writing experience, we are committed to seeing your work printed and your words read!

Writing poetry is an extremely individual and personal process, with few (if any) rules and so, like the previous collections, I have kept almost every piece of poetry exactly as sent, regardless of structure, punctuation, capitalisation etc. This is the poet's work, and not mine to alter! I have also accepted most contributions sent to me, regardless of the writers' skill and experience; my ambitions are to see writers' work published and read, and certainly not to judge, critique or criticize; I have thoroughly enjoyed the naive and simple just as much as the more complex and profound. With the short prose, I have just edited any typos and standardised US grammar to English.

With many of the contributions reflecting the diverse backgrounds and cultures of the writers, in SEASONS there are 119 contributions from 46 writers in 19 countries: Australia, Bahrain, Canada, England, Greece, India, Italy, Malawi, Malaysia, Malta, New Zealand, Northern Ireland, Republic of Ireland, Scotland, South Africa, Sri Lanka, Tanzania, USA and Vietnam, all exploring the seasons – spring, summer, autumn and winter - in their particular country or location.

The Seasons is a unique collection of poetry and short prose from some of the most talented and inspirational writers around the world.

I hope you enjoy this book as much as I have enjoyed putting it together, and if you want to know a little more about any of the writers featured, there is a short biography of almost all of them at the back of the book or online at our website.

Keep on writing!

Best wishes

Robin Barratt
Editor and Publisher
Editor@collectionsofpoetryandprose.com

PS: *If you want to contribute to any of our forthcoming collections, go to the back of this book!*

PPS: *Do treat yourself to a copy of LONELY, LOVE, TRAVEL, WAR, HAPPY and BETRAYAL too, and build up your library of our unique book series! Details... yes, also at the back of this book!*

SPRING

The Bluebell Wood

By Barbara E. Robinson

I feel the warm kiss of sunbeams
through each branch of oak and elm,
as I stroll through a sea of bluebells
whose blossoms now overwhelm
my senses like the touch of Morpheus,
tempting me to keep
my silence by the crystal stream,
to lay my head and sleep.

Bluer than the summer skies,
more vibrant than the sweetest rose,
bluebells ring their beauty now,
woken from their deep repose.
A scene which makes me draw sharp breath
and hold it in deep awe
whilst drinking in this beauteous sight,
I never should crave more.

But times like this I deeply wish
that spring could follow spring,
more days I'd walk the bluebell path
and how my heart would sing.
I feast my eyes upon this fair,
enchanting artist's scene
and wish to hold it's hand forever,
my fragrant Elysian dream.

First published in Metverse Muse magazine, India.

Nature's Symphony

By Tracy Davidson

nature's symphony
the sound of a saxophone
in a bullfrog's croak

The Great Cycle

By Bill Cox

The sun rose, its languid orange rays striking the snow patch that rested just below the summit. The water molecules, energised by the solar rays, experienced a phase change, a radical transformation from the crystal slumber of ice to the flowing excitement of liquid. A small pool collected in a rocky hollow below the snow patch and as the meltwater added to it the pool overflowed, water trickling out and down. The water surrendered to the gentle but unrelenting nagging of universal gravity and began to descend the mountain with a bubbling exuberance.

Above and below ground, burbling through peat and heather, the stream wound its way down through precipitous rocky slopes, enjoying the view from the granite heart of the mountain range. The stream became aware of the animal life around it. Grazing mountain hares, white winter coats now contaminated by brown fur, their bodies acknowledging the onset of spring; red grouse, squawking noisily as their minds incubate the first thoughts of procreation.

Downward the stream flowed, other tributaries joining it in due course, their water just as fresh, just as cold, each hailing the other and finding joy as they added their strength to the flow. The rate of descent slowed as the slopes levelled off, the mountains now towering above the stream on either side, looking paternally down from scree-covered heights.

The current increased and as more streams merged the river finally became aware of itself and stretched, pushing its banks further apart. Life, from micro to macro, took succour from the life-sustaining waters. Infant salmon now swam in it, the shape of its rocky pools imprinted on their piscine memories, creating a bond that would last a lifetime.

The river found the land influencing its emotions. Constriction in its banks created rapids, foaming cascades of violent mania, dangerous to the unwary. These contrasted with the open plains that encouraged a meandering torpor, a sluggishness of current where algae bloomed and exhausted fish rested.

However, these states were passing and eventually the river began to sense a greater truth, hanging like a taste of salt in the air. As snowdrops blossomed in white clusters on its banks, the river found itself bloating out into an estuary where its waters finally met the briny embrace of the world ocean. Mute swans floated majestically by, while redshank waded on the muddy banks, long beaks piercing the damp earth with hungry curiosity. As the days lengthened many birds would find a migratory restlessness harder and harder to ignore, the mental image of distant breeding grounds building within them an urge to inevitable action.

The river approached its mouth, feeling the restless movement of lunar tides brushing its now distant banks, the workings of that same gravitational force that had encouraged its own journey downwards from that distant mountain citadel. Seals, creatures of the sea, paid homage to the river, playfully bobbing and diving in its sheltered waters.

As their two bodies caressed each other, the ocean spoke reassuringly to the river; this is not the end, it said. Water never dies. Look up to the heavens and see your future. Our journey never ends.

The river sat contentedly back and basked in the warm spring sunshine, its waters gently lapping the sandy shore. Soon, a new stage of the journey would begin. The Great Cycle would continue, forever shaping this world and all life on it.

I Reminisce, I Reminisce

By David Watt

I reminisce, I reminisce,
About those springs of old
When life was in its heyday
And days were never cold;
When joy was there for taking,
Plucked from laden branch;
Play was what we made it,
On heels of circumstance.

I reminisce, I reminisce,
Sweet perfumes on the breeze,
Colours of the garden,
The buzzing hum of bees;
Places we would wander
In groups of twos or threes,
With no other purpose
Than afternoons at ease.

I reminisce, I reminisce,
That light of perfect strength,
Warm enough to nourish,
Considerate in length;
Not leading to exertion
When meadows lay to roam,
Trees remained for climbing,
Whole neighbourhood meant home.
I reminisce, I reminisce,
For what may never be;
Return of springs a child
Knew, hopeless now to see;
Cluttered as our minds are
With worries day to day,
Fogs of limitation,
Forgotten rules of play.

Spring Elegy

By Dr. Kapardel Eftichia

Knock on the shoulders wings
Oh! days with fragrant
flowers circled
the fruitfulness of love
the light that always shines in
spring crossing

The veil of dawn
beauty wreaths
the tender shoots and
the fruits of each
generation, overflowing

In the early dew drops
dawn
the naked body
land victorious
buds
pleasure burst

Memories Of Spring

By Sara Madan

Looking through the window she saw the first blooms - roses, asters, bluebells and daffodils. Their fragrance was like a symphony wafting through her memory with the first sign of spring. The flower beds burst into marvellous glory like a painted masterpiece. She thought... if only she could pluck them one by one, she would be in her garden forever.

Remembering her childhood days exploring the enchanting meadows. Picking every flower and dancing in the cool breeze. Sunshine kissing her rosy cheeks while gathering daisies and pansies for a bouquet to her grandmother. She dreamt of faraway lands, and wished that spring would never end. The chirping of sparrows and swaying grass under the pale blue sky made her feel like a fairy on a cloud. Feelings of excitement permeated within; it was always a happy spring. Then came the spring affair, his glance mesmerized her. She stood in awe wondering if two souls could cross the realms of fantasy and become one... It was a new awakening which filled her heart with warmth unlike any other. Rejoicing in his warmth and intoxicating fragrance of lavender. He felt her love like the sun kissed petals. She was his spring and he was her earth. She was like the water that hydrated him in every sphere of his life. She was the one who was everything to him, his beautiful spring.

Death... Then came the time when everything was dust and smog, No roses or jasmines to pluck, or chase the butterflies in the grass. She missed the robins and the sparrows chirp, she was suffocated in the blazing sun. No pleasant breeze, no tender sun kissed morning dew. No blue sky, just a thick blanket of smog. The fire died from his soul, his spring was lost to global warming... The air turned dull, his joys were drowned into sorrows. She was gone forever; his spring was destroyed by the (greenhouse gases). No whiff of flowers, just tears, tears and tears... So in memory she would always be His Spring...

Re-birth... At each dawn he waited for his spring longingly. Wishing she would return once more. He moved from field to field, everything had turned to dust and ashes. His love stood the test of time, for his longing turned to glory. Out of the blue like the fresh morning dew she came like the ray of the sun. Daffodils, Lilacs, Roses and Daisies danced again with their scent in the breeze. Spring strolled on Earth hand in hand happy to be together again. Renewing the hope of rebirth in our lives.

Orchard In Blossom

By Greg Bogaerts

Margaret struggles up the steep track running in loops across the cliff face, breakers boom below her, the force of water makes the rock shudder. For all the violence of the water and the cruel whistling of the wind lashing her brown face with stinging salt, Margaret's eyes droop as though the grind of the elements has almost seduced her into sleep.

On her back is a pack made of hessian bags, sewn together with string, filled with lengths of red and yellow kelp and seaweed like wet broadloom carpet. Margaret can smell the pungent seaweed and kelp and she can feel the spines and thorns through the hessian rubbing through her dress, lacerating some blood from her back arthritis curled.

Margaret goes to the tidal rock platform every day in late winter and early spring and harvests at low tide. She steps down off the platform onto the sand and rock of the sea bottom with the ocean a grey wolf gnashing its teeth in the distance until high tide brings it back licking at Margaret's ankles.

Dragging the hessian pack along she fills it tearing the kelp and weed from the rocks. From underneath the dark secret rock shelves full empty silver abalone shells and crabs that skitter sideways away from the light and the hands of the old woman that reach in, grab hold of seaweed and wrench it triumphantly into daylight.

Margaret works as long as she can but when the icy water reaches up her calves like an old lover made clumsy by disease, she steps back onto the rock platform with the pack of weed, slings it onto her back with the belt of hessian wrapped around her forehead.

She nears the top of the cliff and the belt of hessian, sewn to the sides of the pack, pulls hard against her forehead. But it's the best way to carry the load, the way her great great grandmother carried the loads of coal in Dunfermline in Scotland, scurrying up ladders, going from gallery to gallery with the mined coal in the leather pack. The forehead and neck of the great great grandmother took the weight as well as her back as she moved ever upwards towards the pithead towards the light the leather belt leaving a deep indentation of care and worry in the woman's forehead after years of toil.

Margaret steps out of the shadow darkness of the cliff into the cone of spring light that rages and howls like tundra snow and ice. Margaret smiles, steps into the silent storm of light the way she has for seventy-something seasons. It guides her along the dirt track to her cottage where she unshoulders the pack of weed near the crumbling sandstone front step of her house.

There is time for a cup of tea, Margaret pours the boiling water from the kettle into the pot and the black and blue leaves give up their taste and smell. Tendrils of fragrant steam tangle in the old woman's grey hair when she pours the tea into the metal and enamel cup her husband took with him every day, once upon a time, when he worked in the industries, away from the coast, close to the edge of the city.

Margaret sips it black, sugarless, as bitter as a lonely death in a silent room. Below her, the water of the harbour and the open ocean shifts, breathes, sighs. Distant sounds of city clamour work their way through the air but Margaret does not hear them. She sees the spring light ignite the grass into green flame sloping down to the deep cleft, as dark as black velvet, between two hills.

Sighing, smiling to herself, Margaret swings the kelp and seaweed onto her back, trudges down the slope, green fire shocks and surges around her form making her seem as though she is stepping into another time and place. A place where time has no purchase and death is a black metal key swinging on a ring a hand might reach for easily and find.

The darkness of the shadow cleft between the two hills rises around the old woman, she feels the cold but below her feet, not far away, the three trees, newly budded with blossom, throw bright light into her eyes. They flame like Roman Candles on Cracker Night the blossoms are misty globes of white, yellow and purple lighting the slate black floor of the narrow valley from which the trees grow.

Sliding away the weight of the seaweed, Margaret picks up the pack, shakes the weed and kelp out around the roots of the trees. Taking a garden fork, leaning against one of the trees, she begins to dig in the weed, delving down deep with steel prongs, burying the kelp and weed deep, close to the roots of the trees. The way one of her ancestors buried seaweed in Ireland, during the famine, to enrich the soil to grow potatoes again to feed his family, wretched and starving in their stone hovel near the sea.

The plum tree, bearer of bitter fruit, is Margaret's husband's tree. As she digs the weed around it she sees him coming over the hill red and randy after four glasses of port and coke at the pub after work. She feels his rough and reckless touch upon her old hide and her tears fall.

The apple tree is her child's tree and she sees the infant swaddled in a thick crocheted shawl trimmed with bright silver ribbon. She remembers her confusion, peering closely to discern the features of the baby, and her shame, when she felt relief when it died soon after birth.

The pear tree belongs to Margaret's lover, of many years ago, and she sees him as she digs the golden kelp around the roots. He comes to her now young and hearty, full of health, full of vigour and patience to make her body sing and cry like a mandolin.

Night comes. The woman drags the empty pack out of the cleft and behind her, the blossoms talk to her, beseech her, plead with her, whisper to her and she must struggle to get back to the cottage and the fire waiting in the grate for her.

Arrival Of Spring

By Linda M. Crate

when I hear birdsong break
against the land to nest upon my
ears,
and when the sun withers snow away
to water;
when the baby animals are born
and spring flowers make their arrival
my heart feels full -
winter weariness is washed away
abandoned and forgotten to some place
I cannot and do not wish to
follow,
and I can walk down the sidewalk
without freezing to death
in my journey
wherever I may be going;
and I feel more alive than I did when winter
laughed and cackled with grey clouds of snow
and silence that can cut so viciously like a knife
whose beauty seems to fade after the
first snowfall.

Spring

By Brian Langley

Winter time has come and gone
And spring is here *agen*;
It's come a little early
But it does that now and then.

The birds are nesting in the trees,
The flowers blooming bright;
The days are warm and sunny
But it's chilly stil at night.

For spring, it is a wondrous time;
The air is fresh and clean,
Washed by the winter's falling rains
And grass grows lush and green.

The dams along the creek are full,
There's ducks and ibis there,
And spring, it weaves its magic touch
Around us, everywhere!

Vernal Equinox

By LindaAnn Lo Schiavo

Wind-skinned March, dragon-clawed, maintains its rein
With spiteful shifts of bitter blasts like slaps,
Pretending winter's staying to raid joints,
Crack knees like kindling, or detour lovers
Indoors while it goes whistling past the Ides -
Until the vernal equinox when Sun
Caresses the equator to arouse
Earth, singling out his former partner (cold
At first, hard-crusted), knowing he's approached
Before and, when she warms, spring's miracles
Are easy, marking marriage with day-night
Equals, short-changing lovers of covers
Of darkness, as a slow unfolding light
Stretches, helps April find all that was lost.

First published by *Mused, BellaOnline Literary Review, Winter Solstice* issue, December 2014.

Visions Aspects

By David Hollywood

Visions aspects sculptured years,
Of memories, instructions seared

From views of growth inspired anew,
In mornings when we drank our dew,

And apparitions hopes stayed fresh,
As new days dawning's image met,

Creations from ambitions rest,
Bequeathing scenes, replenished zest.

~

And winter's harvest arbitrates,
To waken lives that conjugates,

Enchanted by a trance thereof,
In slumbered dreams replete with love,

Renewed exhaustions for life's length,
Supporting spring's awakened strength.

The Birds In Spring

By Abigail George

Sometimes things get
lost and a useless feeling you have never experienced
overcomes you.

I want the familiar. The
uninterrupted source. I
think that is why I believe
there is a God. It was

familiar to me when I was a
child deep in thought. Not so

much in high school

when I observed atheism
and agnosticism. Not
really understanding
what they meant like birds in Singapore.

I loved my sadness and
I loved how the walls
were not bright in that room.
They were white and cool
when I touched them with my fingertips.

There were no birds that spring yet.

No garden for them to play in.
No red brick alarming me.
No one waiting for me with vows to be said.
Self-pity was there. I loved
that hollow chocolate Easter egg.
There were no men. There were no women.
No children to make me feel small.
No one to say 'I love you' to me.

I did not have to say those
words back to anyone.
It was bliss. Here I was on
the threshold of bliss.
I knew at the end of the day

I would have an impact on someone's life.

I did not know how or when.
I just knew I had to be ready
And write down these words.

Spring

By Chrys Salt

The street is sudden pink blossom
the pavement a hopscotch of sun
that glitters and skitters down
railings and dances on bumper and pram
in a street of sudden pink blossom.

The trumpet of car horn and drum
of the feet of early commuters
has a beat less wearisome
down a street of sudden pink blossom
(surely yesterday's branches were bare?).
Spring arrived overnight with a blush on
and flowers in her hair.

Snowfall, April

By Mantz Yorke

Alarm... 6.45:
brightness edging the curtains
when I'd expected dark.
Snow lying lightly

under clear skies has thinned
the cherry trees' oranges
and pinks to fluorescence.
On these bursting buds

lie clusters of soft dragees,
unsilvered and translucent,
cold-blooded spiderlings
waiting for the sun.

April Memory

By Mary Anne Zammit

When we have met
It was spring.
When your lips reached for mine.
Love made its best deal.
Under the April skies.

My heart resides besides the green meadows.
We have loved
All flowers blossomed.
Trees got greener,
and the sun have finally found us.

Standing at the fields
My heart is awakened.
And I will wait
for another April,
for spring.
For you.

May

By Dr. Kapardeli Eftichia

Small joys of May
butterflies inside
blossom leaves
boats with sails open like
Mind and heart
touch the stars
like free birds
stand

Small joys of May
carefree small brides
under the same sky
flushed cheeks
flowers expensive
in lips
painted, defenceless
in love

Small joys of May
sweet drops beauty
lily blossoms and
the thoughts spread like
gold ivy
glide to light
desperately

Early Plum Blossom

By Tracy Davidson

early plum blossom
his whispered conversations
to our unborn son

Antipodes

By Jennifer Riggs

At start of year in climes down under
Ozzies bask while cold Poms chunder –
Is it some gigantic cosmic blunder?
No, semper Australia floribunda.

Autumn is just a ten-day wonder –
No risk of snow, small risk of thunder.

In wintertime in southern latitude
We are at risk from duck-billed platitude
As, murmuring our eternal gratitude,
We still maintain our basking attitude.

Welcoming spring with more beatitude:
Praise the Lord for our great climatitude!

Veld Lily & Frida Kahlo

By Kathleen Bleakley

Veld Lily, your roots
in the same continent
as mine, Africa
yours South, mine North

Veld Lily, Sand Onion
growing in arid soils
flowering with spring rain

you take me back
dusky red deserts
palmeries, dates, figs
fields of broad beans and chick peas
your pink tubes
the colour of Marrakesh
stone buildings, rose gardens

your blooms, shapes of red hot pokers
succulent, shiny leaves
bold as Frida Kahlo's paintings
watermelon, papaya, bananas
cacti, bird of paradise

Veld Lily, I've chosen colours for Frida
musk through to fire
leaf patterns, she too a wildflower
blooming, through disease and accident

I'm wearing Frida's kaleidoscopic jewels
seeing her dreams, gardens, jungles
remembering Barbary apes in Morocco
scampering in cedar forests

Vervet monkeys, silvery grey
old worlds
Veld Lily, we are far
from when
Australia and Africa were one
in Gondwanaland

First published in *New Shoots Poetry Anthology*, Red Room Company & Rochford St Review, 2017

Mysterious States Of America

By John Tunaley

After first rain, newly ploughed prairie smells
Sweet as a nut. Hazel? Walnut? Not quite...
Perhaps sesame? Anyhow it spells
'Fertile.' Soon cylindrical catlinite
Potatoes will heave rich white-gleamed jasper
And cherry gems; their eyes blinking dark
Powder-horns in the night. As per
Usual unembarrassed, a cold stark
Pole star hangs up there; cosmic, faithful... proud.
Flat lakes of red-gold carp mutter and moan...
Yellow panthers under isles of grey cloud
Lap medicinal waters. Lap and groan.

On a brown skyline, taut as a stretched bowstring,
Sway bear and moose. They appear to be dancing.

Spring

By Rebecca Sutton

Spring is boring,
nothing seems to happen.
The sun is hardly ever here,
and the snow has quickly disappeared.

Spring is not really a season,
it is just a transition
from winter to summer.
Spring is neither hot nor is it cold,
so I wonder, why is it even here.

Late Spring With Bogongs

By John Karl Stokes

They're like eating fat
rock
granite ripples
moth-carved
a million tickles
in the mouth
you strip the wings
bite down on nut
- oiled flesh
they taste...

like moths
You can gulp
like a native
slapping feet
on stone
bellies sweat
light, leave
your mark in every
bite, play
at time's menu:

a mouthful
of whirred suns.

First published in *Fire in the Afternoon*, Halstead Press 2014.

Spring Babies

By Clare Roslington

Our beautiful angel babies
Are coming in the spring
To welcome the season of new life in
With gentle love and perfect grace
They will come from my nurturing womb
Into our nurturing embrace

As the daffodils show their golden face
And all the leaves emerge from bud
The blossom on the trees
Blooming in pure white to reflect their angelic beauty

All around vitality springs up from mother earth's lap
As our vibrant children sit on our loving lap
Always held in our tender heart
We shall nurture and cherish our beloved baby angels
With the grace of pure devotion
Tending to our happy love family

Everyone who comes to visit will be bathed in purest love
And when it's time to go they will depart
With a happy gentle smile
And loving warmth in their heart

Our friends and family love and nurture us
As we love and nourish our beloved angel twins
All smiling and peaceful so loved from deep within
Our heart and soul
That unite forever as one
In the grace of the highest spiritual sun

Moving Force

By Bernadette Perez

The wind blows hard
lifts matter in the yard
Twirling branches in the breeze
gathers obstacles piece by piece
Scattered fragments flock like geese

I'd think twice
before I'd stroll

decide which way to go
Vision profiled by desire
waits to ignite the fire

Out of control
life takes a toll
My mind is mangled
thoughts therefore tangled
Detour- produce a clearing
mass construct on detained
Distraction visibly tamed

Frazzled pictures from the past
Imprint memories that may pass
Dust gathers between location
dirt trapped within space relocated
Piled high in a disorderly fashion
watch as it tumbles down
Sporadic reaction

Still and calm
pressured air release
Burst
out comes rain
Set free the beast
that brings terror's reign

Forcing through an open passage
Dramatic entrance at view
duck and hide
Come out to play
Soon you too will be blow away

I travel in the wind
A force to reckon with
No longer bound
No where to be found
On a mission
Life begins to spin
Moving
Moving
Moving
A Blissful transition to an end

Gentle Rain

By Dr. Kapardeli Eftichia

Through the thin shadow
the small cloud
a sudden peaceful, humble
spring gentle ra n
irrigates the soil.

From music and
frantic dance
the most
small forgotten
grass awakening
are delivered, thirstily.

In this hugging the
full of smells
Sun lowers
smiling again winner
the calcined stones
the rain thousards of kisses
he had left.

Spring

By Lynette Cupido

The season where flowers start to bloom,
The season for the sun to shine.
The cold has left the grey, love has gone
And forgotten.
The season of new love too,
Blooms as the flowers on the trees.
This season find someone who can take
Care of your soul and heart,,
Good or bad, it's the experience and
A lesson to be learned.
The gentle rain from heaven
That washes away all pain.
The rain brings cleanliness, new beginnings,
New flowers, leaves.
New love and positivity.
Spring, a time to rejoice.
Believe in beauty,
Respecting,
And believe that God
Created everything.

Mad March At Daybreak

By LindaAnn Lo Schiavo

Manhattan's mad March broadcasts misery,
Sharp air invasive as heartaches. You left.

Solidity gone, daybreak kicks me out
Of bed. I run through stark parks, jogging past
Low snow-fat branches crinkling from a dance
Of chickadees acquainted with mistakes
And concepts of good timing. Single-file,
Negotiating severed roots, I move
As twig-filled light ahead speaks privately
To me in blue sky language: "Yes," it says
Today, "old mud remains. But a cold spell
Is fading. Spring's when gravity begins
Reversing, when vines climb deserted walls,
When woods swell to desired darkness while
Earth's creatures mate." Weight shifts. That smooth hold is
Returning. I almost sense blossoming -
Tender bits flowering behind my back.

The Feral Cat

By Gabriella Garofalo

Too soon you lost your innocence,
My feral cat that sneers at those daft cherry blossoms
And the broken smiles the sun feels bound to show -
My feral cat that gave me birth, my soul, my season,
My feral cat that whispers she plans to strike limbs and leaves,
Mid April, a demise, while patsies dream
Leaves and limbs won't die -
Well, folks, they do, that's why I always listen,
That's why the weirdest prayers crowd my mind at night:
Time of whatever month, time of whatever hour,
Have mercy on my feral cat, never mind the trees,
They're tougher than us twins, aren't they,
What with those ancient roots, intrusive branches,
The shadows of a cheap foliage -
Sorry? What do you mean? Oh, I see, you can't,
Only black in stock today,
OK, my feral cat and I'll grab and wrench
Flowers, dreams, roots, stop that bloody swanking
Then we'll dive into the waves -
Who says feral cats loathe the wild white foams
Where words and smiles crave to crash and drown,
High time for them, high time for us,
My feral cat, my spring -
April, our heartfelt thanks for sparing crooked old souls,
Stealing life in bud works better, right?
Thanks a lot, you bloody month, for being so kind:
Well, afraid we must be leaving now
Our bosom friends are waiting,
Too small for you to see and swallow 'em.

Spring! Spring! Spring!

By Akanksha Bhatnagar

The season was spring
Smile on everyone's face it did bring
Gone to grandma's home
My childhood love began
Spring! Spring! Spring!

Nothing was so beautiful as spring
The time, when I got my wing
My soul acted like butterfly
My love for him was so high
Spring! Spring! Spring!

That special day was only in spring
My soul started to sing
A quivering leaf in the wake of rain
A heart to lose, a soul to gain
Spring! Spring! Spring!

Days were blossoming
That smile was so killing
My inner bird eagerly wanted to fly
My outer looks stopped me from going to sky
Spring! Spring! Spring!

Those memories still ping
Mind has stopped, but heart is waiting
The loveable time has passed
But memories aren't last
Spring! Spring! Spring!

SUMMER

Summer Days

By Brian Langley

Now summer's here, we all go off
Down to the ocean blue.
To frolic in the icy waves.
And catch a dose of flu.

Then out we get and sit and cook
Our bodies in the sun.
We lie there soaking up the rays
Till we are overdone.

We eat a meal of fish and chips
Cooked in loads of fat.
We like to think it's healthy.
But I'm not so sure of that.

The kid goes playing on the rocks
And falls and busts his knees.
We take him to the doctor
And cant afford the fees

And then we have a slow trip home
Along with all the others
Who've spent the day out having fun
With children, wives and mothers.

And so, next day, it's off to work.
I cough, I'm sore, I'm broke.
I tell my mates we had such fun.
It's really quite a joke

For I'd sooner watch the cricket
On the TV in my den.
But I suppose, come next weekend
We'll do it all again.

The Ghost In Cabin 5

By Rosemary Rigsby

Winter crept in after autumn caught me surprised and unprepared. Summer's triumphs had felt infinite, and I hadn't thought about the dark days ahead. The dark days are here, despite this room's pallid light, its cool white walls, and another silver dawn beyond the window. I am weary of the knife-edged dark, unrelieved by counterfeit glare. Summer glows far ahead. And farther back. I look through the pa e window and feel that glow pulling me, pulling me from whiteness to warmth, to summer and Cabin 5.

My husband and I retreat to Cabin 5 every year; a summer sojourn that we have shared with our parents, siblings, children, grandchildren. We swim, we fish and we eat too many hot dogs. On laid-back afternoons, we count the loons on the lake. We lounge in dry wooden chairs on the cabin's scrubby lawn. The lawn is mostly anthill, but we don't mind. I flick wayward ants while I read languid fiction, magazine fluff, or dusty pocketbooks from the local thrift shop. I have my sketch book and pencils, and camera. We live in Cabin 5 as if each day is our last.

There are other cabins, but Cabin 5 is the one that holds our memories. Other memories probably dwell there too, as it is over 100 years old. The region's earliest, and hardiest, pioneers built the cabin. They put in a garden and farmed the land sloping up from the lake. Later owners built more log houses where sightseers sought wilderness adventures. When a forest fire swept through the property, most of the cabins went up in flames, but somehow Cabin 5, and its ghosts, survived.

This summer we drive down the hill and there it is – the squat cabin facing the lake. The fir tree in front has grown wider, but the birch on the edge of the beach is gone. A grey stump remains. A red metal roof has replaced the mossy, and leaky, shingles, and fresh white chinking fills the spaces between the blackening logs. A new casement window winks back in the setting sun.

A family of Canada geese stroll across the yard with soft honks, intent and dignified. They ignore our car pulling up beside the cabin. I remember my parents' terrier straining at her leash, desperate to put the run on the trespassing geese. She was a feisty little dog, but is long gone. Mum and dad came here often, and once we hosted all of our parents and siblings for a hilarious week of family food gatherings and campfire marshmallows. We all swam, walked the trails around the lake, read books and worked puzzles. The grandchildren came later, bringing wonder and promise.

Out on the lake, two paddlers in a canoe send a wedge of

waning ripples across the lake. At the dock, a black Labrador retriever stands in a rowboat. He looks like our old dog, but all Labs look a lot alike. The dog barks and waves his tail as a man shoves the boat free and takes the oars.

I remember our son's motorboat and how much he loved to waterski. One time when he skied, his sister drove, and I spotted. I can still feel my hair whipping my face and hear the cheers from the beach as he slalomed past, spraying water over his fan-club. Once, in a family cavalcade, we launched two boats for a cruise in beaming sunshine and sparkling waves. We tied up in a secret cove and ate our lunch on the beach - sandwiches, fruit and a lake-full of cold water. Our daughter-in-law had packed cinnamon buns, but our grandson dropped his in the sand. He was too big for tears, but his auntie, who had baked the goodies, found him another.

I step onto the porch. This is where another of our grandsons played with his toy dump trucks and diggers, singing *The Wheels on the Bus*, as he dumped gravel on the steps and pushed it off with his grader. He and his sister swam in the lake with their floaties - a frog for him and a swan for her. She pulled a waterlily and tied it over her ear. We called her Princess Waterlily. All of the children fished from the wharf with child-sized rods and with help from their grandfather, while their mothers set the picnic table with buns, pickles, and tomatoes. We knew there would be no fish, but when they straggled home, Grampa would be in charge of the hot dogs on the barbecue. The kids laughed and screeched as they hooked water weeds and lily pads. They cried when it was time to leave Cabin 5.

We loved having our family around us in this temporal place, but sometimes my husband and I had the cabin to ourselves for a few days of lazy lie-ins. We listened to the loons' lingering calls and breathed lily-scented air borne on the morning breeze. Some mornings, I let him sleep. Dew dampened bare ankles as I walked down to the shore and sat cross-legged on the dock. I watched the sun rise behind the far mountain, its peak a wavering reflection on the silent lake, seen through tears.

I pass through the front door.

I hear children's laughter, but all of our grandchildren are grown. A little girl crayons at the kitchen table, and a small boy dashes past me with a giant beach ball. He doesn't even glance at me. A woman stands at the counter slicing cucumbers and tomatoes. Gleaming steaks, salted and peppered, wait for the barbecue. I reach for her. I want to touch her and let her know I am here. From outside, a man's voice asks if he should light the barbie now. The woman turns and laughs. *Yes, please*, she says. A film, a haze surrounds her. She fades, ghost-like. I open my mouth, but nothing comes out.

I look over my shoulder. My husband should be right behind me with baggage in his arms. I step outside, then turn and look at Cabin 5, but I am lifted away. Cabin 5, and all of its ghosts, whirls at the bottom of an eddy of mist. I am the ghost. The ghost is me.

Hedgerows

By Terry Hickland

The old man walks at a laboured pace, face weathered and worn. Thin, exhausted frame, clothed in worn baggy shirt and trousers, unkempt grey hair creeping out from beneath his threadbare cap.

Council worker they call him, as he makes his way along the rural lane. The shine of his high-laced black boots seems out of place on the greying tarmac.

A faded, Sam Brown belt around his waist acts as a scabbard. A humble sickle hangs from it like a lone assassin. Merrily it jangles against the battered and blackened tea can, announcing his presence to no one in particular.

A macabre figure, scythe slung over a gnarled and worn shoulder, looks for a likely mound of earth where the cull will begin.

Tools for a moment discarded, small fire set to raise a welcome brew, its aroma carried along on the soft morning breeze.

Amorous swallows call out overhead, vying for one another's attention, oblivious to mankind's existence.

Balancing a box on his knee, calloused hands delicately roll a cigarette, to be sealed with a gentle swipe of his tongue.

Refreshed from his only vice, he finishes the sweet tea, rises to his feet, cap tilted. The blade of the scythe makes little sound, the trusted sandstone providing a razor's edge.

In his battle with nature, the indigenous growth has been curtailed for now.

Hot
By Bernadette Ferez

I rest under the maple tree
Heat overwhelming
Sweat drips from brow
Blinding me
Like dew puddles sitting on petals
Bursting from the leaves

The hottest day is still to come
Temperatures a rising
Degrees of burning bud
Passion becomes sticky
In sunshine splashing water is fun

Enjoy lunch less formal
Picnic at park
Laughter of children playing
Musical influenced performance
Dramatic engag ng pretences

Tea parties for imaginary friends
Hide and seek
Tag your it

Sky filled with toys
Framed man-made material
Light weight flowing
Colours of design turning patterns up above
A gentle breeze cools
This is summer
Hot uncomfortable intense
Boiling calmness

Supremacy Of Summer

By David Watt

Summer, endless summer – if only it could be!
The chirrup of cicadas rejoicing under tree,
Sweet somnolence of sunlight, lulling mind until
Sunset's gold upholstery dips 'neath distant hill.

Dinners on veranda, cool drinks tantalising,
Balmy breezes harmonised to sway of socialising;
Time to send your worries away on holiday
To chill as distant memories, bleak, and icy grey.

And ripened to their fullness hang apricot, then pear,
Seducing taste with perfume drawn from summer air,
Providing depth of sweetness her warmth may only bring,
Causing heart to gladden, contented lips to sing.

Just to prove for certain that summer reigns supreme,
Above the other seasons prone to wild extreme;
Summer nights stay modest, dipping none-too low,
Languid days make contrast to coming times of snow.

Lament Of A Late Riser

By Barbara E. Robinson

And had I remembered
what beauty lay in store
I would surely have risen sooner,
maybe one hour before
the dawn when flowers opened petals
to the morning mist,
their pretty heads raised ready
with sparkling dew to be kissed.
Would then the heron have waded
breaking his dense cover,
the early fisher of the river
standing first or one leg then the other?
Oh tardy one was I who lay
neath covers buried like a mole
so missing those sights that are
the food and drink of a peaceful soul.

Did squirrel twitch his nose
to scent any danger in the air
and has fox gone skulking back
to her young cubs in hidden lair?
Did the perfume of the wild rose hedge
rival that of new mown hay
or reflections on the water dance
with the fishes at their play?
Gone distant call of cuckoo
seeking other's homely nest
wherein to lay her egg and flee
leaving uninvited guest.
Oh languid soul, oh slothful one
was I from sheets quite loath to part
so missing the sights that would have been
sweet music to my heart.

First published in Indigo Dreams' 'REACH' magazine

Middle Earth

By Stella Carruthers

It's a lisping breath hot-sticking-thighs-to-a-leather-seat kind of day. A day where I walk in canvas high-top sneakers, painted with flowers and inked with vivid pen, up the hill towards The Peak. I pass houses with paint-peel-away-walls. They look like how I feel. Kind of fragile and desperate to get past the shallow colours to something deeper, more real, maybe more meaningful. The boards of manuka and pine are different shades. One a wood of this native land and the other an import. Like me. Heart born and physical bodied here in these islands but with a longing for the purple lands of my ancestors where they weave boxed fabrics and speak with a lilt and burr.

I head up past these houses. The peeling ones. And the newly minted. There's the track. Almost hidden beside the metal corroded playground. Its sign blending into the woodland. I start to climb. Watching for bikers careering down the steep tracks. I begin to breathe heavily as the incline becomes almost vertical. Around me, yellow flowers and their spiked bushes.

Pausing for water, I sip the now luke-warm liquid from my plastic bottle and wish I'd invested in a metal one. Eco values aside, it, at least would have kept the water cool. I keep climbing and reach the top of the track, having met not another soul. No team of cyclists. Not even another lone walker. Like me.

Bending to touch my toes, stretching my hammies, I stand up and look around at the panoramic view. Across Strait to island in The South. To the wind farm across the hills, white blades cutting the air into thick blue slices. And to the right; to wild coast where, as a child, I bathed in white knickers and singlet in the rock pools, searching for the dark shapes of stars.

I sit on the bench dedicated in death to Adrian (he loved this view) and unwrap my lunch. Knob of yeasty brown bread baked yesterday by myself. Cheese, local, from up The Coast. Stone fruit from orchards down in Central. I eat. Slowly. Savouring each bite. I toss the stone of my apricot down into the gorse. It lies, like a pitted heart, beside the World War II bunker. This concrete structure almost overgrown by grass and gorse. I imagine staying up here. Sleeping under the Southern Cross. Sheltering from Southerly under concrete marked two toned by the reaching hands of lichen. How I would never return to the Glass Towers and black crowds of The City that I see stretching in sparkling expanse below me.

My one piece of civilisation is the cell phone tower, heavy and dark, pointed above me with barbed wire biting the air around it. It's ugly. But makes the view somehow even more beautiful. This mountain peak. A shadow that lies tall and dark on the edge of a city that now half disappears into the noon-day heat.

The sh mmer of warm air feels almost solid. The most solid thing around me with the blue seas and even bluer skies in one direction and ːhe fading city to the other. And me, just a skinny singleted girl, sweat-stuck and smiling, sitting right there in the middle.

Sydney Blue Sky

By Mavis Atha

How do you describe a Sydney blue sky
On this special subject I really will try
To make such a scene visible to someone whose blind
To do so, I know would be very kind

It's like the salt on hot chips or something that's bland
Paddling in sea; running your fingers through sand!
Enjoying a curry instead of boiled fish
A blue sky for everyone that is my wish.

It's the chimes of the bellbirds in the tree tips,
Magnificent music of Chopin or Liszt
Smelling fresh air when leaving the zoo,
Friendship that's shared between me and you.

Gentle breeze wafting over the bay
Heat of the sun on your skin where you lay.
Taste of fresh juice when cooled with ice.
A refreshing shower and watermelon slice!

When the clouds are all gone and the sky is blue,
The sun is shining everything looks brand new,
It makes you feel happy and bright as can be
Enjoying the day, that's what I want you to 'see'.

Summer Rain

By David Watt

Summer rain falls welcome as a present,
Wrapped in silver, pure tasting, elegant;
Bringing that desired of each shower,
Cooling draught for every beast and flower;

But when her precious tears refuse to flow
And weeks turn into month with nought to show,
We look upon the skies with pensive eye
For hint of cloud amid the sunburnt sky.

And nothing fills our mind as does the wish
That once again we hear the silver swish
Of raindrops dressed as only Nature may,
In style never dated, flecked lustrous grey;
For then in her sweet presence may we rest,
Content in certain knowledge we are blessed!

Reverence For Life

By Clare Roslington

As the land begins to cooL
At the ending of a hot summer's day
I walk alone up the steep hill
To connect with the Earth
And with myself

My heart quickens with the vibrant energy
Of aliveness
Gradually as I climb higher
My breath becomes deeper
Softening as my mind starts to calm
And listen to the sounds all around

A sudden movement of a rabbit brings me fully present
Pure gratitude and joy fills my heart
Knowing I made the right choice to come here tonight
The air is clear here
The clarity and the calm breath
Brings me home to my true self
Beyond the stories and worries

I sit and look out upon the lush green lands
And the soft purple tinged outline of the Welsh hills
A hand on my heart
I give thanks for my life, my blessings of love and family
Of peace and compassion
And acceptance of my failings
My heart trusts that all is well
In this moment of beauty

The orange sun glides down to touch the earth
As I walk filled with joy
And reverence for all life
Upon these beautiful hills, my home

Let This Summer Be Warm

By Linda M. Crate

all this spring rain
makes me eager for
a warmer summer
not burn the skin off the bone
boiling hot
kind of summer
but one that doesn't make me
shiver or wear coats
the entire time;
one that is kinder than this cold
silver rain falling upon the skin in a
hard kiss against my
flesh -
if it must rain then let it be warm
reviving to the bones
all things that winter tried to steal
from them
and let me be kissed by summer flowers
wild and domesticated both
making a beautiful, fragrant sea around me
an embrace of both beauty and sweetness

Purple Basil

By Kathleen Bleakley
For my sister Kerstie (18/12/72 – 29/3/11)

Summer brings basil
purple, your favourite colour
days are fragrant
long and humid with grief
tomatoes ripen slowly
so much rain
our sweet corn grows taller
than ever

you've missed the broad beans
you loved to steam
they'll return next spring
if only you could
we would share this harvest
with you

Previously published in *Lightseekers*, poetry by Kathleen Bleakley & images by 'pling, Ginninderra Press, 2015, and *Writing To The Edge*, Spineless Wonders, 2014.

Summer

By Dr. Kapardeli Eftichia

Summertime, white birds
sculptured beaches, oracles of love

Wave of the sea wave multiply
salt shivering die out in the Sun Fire

Sensual bodies, lost in the arms
the day that does not die out

In red nets on the sand of summer
prisoner, a shooting star

Sink in the sun, the sky
the wing of the bird, carve

Blonde teens, blue angels, naked
in the hot sand, fall in love

Joys Of The Season

By Bill Cox

Hay Fever, you are
An affront to my self-image;
The confident outdoorsman
Brought low by invisible grains of pollen,
Microscopic assassins of my ego.
My face is the front line,
The battleground where
My immune system has declared war
On an enemy who needn't have been.
An act of unnecessary hostility,
That results in moist, twitching eyes,
Itchy mouth, tickly cough,
Running nose and gut-wrenching sneezes.
July, the best of summer months
And I just wish to cower,
In a cool, darkened room,
Hiding from an infinite army
Of miniscule grassy fiends
Whose only aim
Is to reduce me
To complete
And utter
Misery.

Hot Sun

By Rebecca Sutton

The sun in the early summertime
is hot and long.
Sometimes way too long.
With my sweat glands now rising
and my skin slowly roasting,
I feel the onset of the summer sun.

Everything dries from the grass to my lips.
I pray for all sorts of wind
to cool down my heat-infused body.
The sweat, the dryness, yet...
the days are longer, the colours are brighter
and I always wake up with a smile on face.

West Coast Witblits

By Justin Fox

Peeling back the long and scrubby West Coast road,
a Beetle stuffed with boards and Tracey babe,
through Tableview, 'Blue Berg' and 'Milk Bush'
with skanking palms and scruff-necked surf
to Koeberg's twin-tit towers that leak electric milk
from concrete pods beside the forests of kelp.
We pass the wind-scoured flats of 'Silver Stream',
'Buck Point' and 'Goose Kraal' to Yzerfontein
whose steely cape takes big swells on the nose
and delights a school of black-finned grommets.

To a beach house that's white from outside to
in, a boardwalk over dunes to a half-moon strand
strung with seaweed, sea wrack and sea foam,
and the waves tall white and giving fright.
We retreat to a cove where bearded hippies
ride the faces of teetering monsters and
oystercatchers dance an orange-legged jig
as surf invades their mussel-bound home.

A summer morning dawns misty cool
soon steaming off to wobbling swelter,
we fly the arrow road to Langebaan
past shallows stained flamingo pink
and clouds that promise waxing southeaster
to a beach where newbie acolytes of wind
practise their flying, gybing, their clumsy
balance and tumble in translucent green.

We pick our boards and rigs, Tracey her floater
'for the porpoises of learning', me a sinker with 6.4
for fast flight across an emerald lagoon
chasing tails of warriors sparring with the wind.
We cleave from chop to trough, drawing parabolas
towards a Postberg shore, there to rest in shallows,
our flesh sun-bronzed, our hair white-blond,
bobbing on our boards in Meeuw Island's lee
watched by gulls and cormorants that reek,
then tearing back to shore in a growing gale,
the crests sleet-torn to a million rags of white.

A windless morn for honing stand-up-paddling skills
not yet extant as we take our acrobatic falls,
giggling through contortions of indignity,
supping from the cup of Langebaan Lagoon.
We pack the car and gun it north to Velddrif where
the Berg River pours through salty flats to Laaiplek,
along a low shore via Dwarskersbos and Rocherpan
with a pale-placid sea and shrill raptors on the wing,
issuing us through the sands of Soutkuil and Brakpan,
hinting at the drought that roasts this land
where I want trance and Tracey Duran Duran,
so we listen instead to the tyre-dirt band.

Over Baboon Mountain and through a lost-forgotten
marsh rimmed by reeds and thatched *langhuisies*
that remind of a time when Dutch farmers took
this Verlorenvlei from its keepers, the Khoisan,
and gave it over to the humble earth-apple for keeps.
We check in to echoing E-Bay hotel, 1950s style,
unchanged in linoleum and doily time warp –
no Garden Route ponce on this course-grained coast.
Our room reeks of fish, smashed windows leak
southeaster and mozzies in Messerschmitt formation.

I rig up beside the caravan park. Faithful Tracey
(long lens and bikini) records for Instagram posterity.
Bearing my sailboard to the font of Atlantic wisdom
or similar Zen, I climb on and groove out through
regimented lines of Weskus flawlessness, leaping lips,
riding green brandy snaps, punched by haymaker gusts,
howling, carving, singing the tune of an E-Bay break
that's pure witblits for the soul or some such mind buchu,
but, oh my hat (!), it's *moer* intoxicating to be pseudo young
and almost free and riding the West Coast rollercoaster.

After such wave bliss I'm limp as a vinegared chip,
so we stroll along the rocky shore and up to a cave
where San once painted eland, Khoi left handprints
and modern vandals scratched their marks
in time's red-fanged autocracy.
Beside the cave, the remains of World War II radar
set to spy for U-boats, bring depth-charging Valkyries
from Langebaan or Ysterplaat to chase the Hun
from our surf spots: *fokof,* locals only, even back then.

In the hotel's cavernous dining hall, his and hers
prawns and calamari with tangy tartar sauce,
Darling Cellars' crisp and peachy Chenin plonk
and enough chips to set us right for another wave.
After supper, the Wit Mossel surfers' pub
where blondes and rats drink cheap wine,
smoke deep zol in a shack hung with dream -
catchers, surfer art and longboards in the rafters.

North we ride through seared lands cracking
under a white sun where ostriches and cows
stand forlorn in dried-up dams, but over a rise
the endless invitation draws us back to the altar.
At Farmer Burger's legendary spot,
a surf hut for hire on a sandstone kop
that overlooks a sweep of coast *sauvage*.
The *hokkie* is all shipwreck chic with seashells,
succulents, a bathroom set in ochre rock
and makeshift Jacuzzi fed by donkey burner
where we wallow pale naked into nights
fuelled by wine and sausage and off the grid,
the soft-hollow thunder of faraway surf
and fantastical Milky Wave breaking overhead.

We rumble into Lambert's metropole
to check out the action, the fish factory,
the sacred *fokol*-ness of this dozy town
and I ride my last wave at Yo-yo Reef
with pods of locals, some going right, me left,
on a break that's all soda fizz and playful slap:
hard strokes, crouch, drop, slice the turn
into a ball and flat out down the line,
a cyan wall curling up, up and ever over.

Oh no! Tracey honks the Beetle's horn,
Cape Town waves its toothy hand and,
electric, I surf a foamy to the beach,
trudge back along the squeaking sand,
toss suit and board in boot and join
the long gravel road south, back down
Africa's sunburnt shin, past Elands Bay
and Dwarskersbos, Velddrif, Langebaan
and Yzerfontein, to concrete Cape Frown
where screen-faced punters squander their days
commuting, grafting, watching the SABC

and surfing their lives away on Facebook.

* Witblits - firewater, moonshine

Summer Thirteen

By Pamela Scott

I remember turning thirteen that summer,
that magical young-old age.
I'm too old to play with Barbie
but too young to make my own decisions.

I've stopped reading my Enid Blyton's
and branched out to Point Horror.
My dolls and toys no longer interest me
and I want to know what the world's like.

In the picture I'm sitting with Dad,
on a wall with the family dog, Marcus.
I look like every other teenage girl
and can't wait to be a grown-up.

I'm dressed like a tom-boy –
blue jeans and a white polo shirt.
I'm holding a can of tango in my hands
and grinning broadly at the camera.

Dad's got on big black sunglasses
and is pretending he's James Dean or something.
I'm patting Marcus's head and
my whole life lies in front of me.

I don't even recognise myself.
I'm not the girl in the picture anymore.
I don't even know who she is
and it's like looking at the image of a stranger.

I'm all grown up now and I've
changed so much from that little girl.
She's completely separate from me
and I doubt if I was ever her.

It took me a long time to get here.
It cost a lot of blood, sweat and tears.
I'm all grown up now and memories
of that girl have faded to black.

A Summertime Of Sharing

By Clare Roslington

Every day we begin anew
Happiness is the grace between me and you
This summer we choose a life of sharing
Abundance of kindness, compassion and caring
To shine our light like the summer sun
Shines upon everyone

Let's give to our children and every friend who we meet
A gentle heart embrace and maybe a piece of cake
Knowing the love inside everyone is always awake
When each person feels held and loved
They can become more
And every aspect of life is adored

The grace of giving is the highest way
To create happiness and harmony
In our beautiful community
Let's all love and be kind to one another
Shine our light day and night
Make kind choices that make our hearts sing
And create a new way together
In this summert me of sharing

Diamond Hill, Connemara National Park

By Mantz Yorke

Blue sky; fair-weather cumulus;
no likelihood of rain. We check in,
then curve up Diamond Hill.
Too roundabout, so we cut direct.
Bad choice. The tawny tussocks
make it a struggle to the top.
We picnic looking across to hills
and down to a tree-lined stream.

'E-elp' sounds faintly on the air.
A person, or just a bleat?
Did Ann hear a shout? No, only sheep.
The faint call again, somewhere below:
I still can't decide – someone or sheep?
Across the valley, two tiny figures
are climbing: dark heads turn pink –
not for a bleating sheep, I think.

I descend, better to see the stream.
No-one visible, but I shout anyway.
No reply, but the distant pair,
now on the shoulder of their hill,
again turn towards the sound,
then disappear from view.
I move down the steepening slope,
call once more. There's no response.

Later we check out, telling the clerk
we thought we'd heard a call
but no-one had shouted back.
"If a car's left in the park, I'll call out
searchers," he says. "But probably not.
A woman signed out minutes ago:
the backs of her fleece and slacks
were wet. I thought it odd, that."

In Love With Summer

By S'busiso Manqa

She's in love
With the warmth of summer,
The clear skies
But not the flies.

When it's hot,
She is hot,
With countless outfits
Complimented by the calendar.

When night falls,
She lives on
Beneath a bliss of stars
Celebrating her freedom.

She's in love
With the warmth of summer,
Warming up her heart
As she hopes for love.

Terrigal

By Mavis Atha

Terrigal... Sharp in the sunshine
Seagulls sweeping over the cricket green.
Restless tourists finding their next parking spot.
Sleepy houses nestling close to their rocky habitat.
Pretty beaches and rocky seashore,
A feast for any budding artist
with pen and canvas poised.
At every turn a picture worth the time,
To sit or stand a while and enjoy
While foam rides on the sea
cleansing the sand with frothy spray.
Cooling breezes round the rock pools play.
Norfolk pines stand firm at the water's edge
Adding dignity and splendour to this place.

For those who like an active kind of life,
There's the water, sparkling and warm.
Surfers and swimmers every season
Enjoy the safe, secluded beach in every way.
Scuba divers with their little craft
All white and brilliant, bobbing on the sea.
Fishermen's boats with tackle to be bought
Enjoy this haven 'far from madding crowd'.

Those who prefer a rock climb or a jog
or just a 'little' walk right up the hill
With views that can surpass most anywhere
Yes - Terrigal is a pretty place!

Tracking

By Barbara E. Robinson

It was my turn to be the bait,
to race away and lose the pack;
leave a trail of twiggy arrows,
message small piles of leaves.
When I raced down the worn track
I hadn't meant to see the world
through overgrown hawthorn,
brambles, and broom so blown
it was taller than me.
But I was a tenacious child,
fought my way through
a screen of twigs, thorns, leaves.
The intrepid explorer
but now the hunted.

Crouched low off track
on hands and knees I stopped
now staring...eye to eye with nature.
Stoat and child, child and stoat
both mesmerized and wary
his black tipped tail, soft fur,
enwrapping thoughts of wonder.
I was snared w thin his eyes...
until the hunters' cries rang out
much clearer now... tracking, trailing.
Stalemate no longer an option
I blinked then slowly retreated
bowing to majesty rarely seen.

Placed 3rd in the Salopeot Members 2011 Competition

Summering Over

By John Karl Stokes

At lake's tolling, they would cross the square
their white shirts shining
We knew all their faces then, barely names;
Manning Clark's hat (following Manning Clark)
The infamously un-named academic (ego-fuzz)
Morris black backed, sleek in her jingling bare feet
A brass band for Brissenden –
Short, satisfactory glimpses, that was it
to be had for sustainment in those summer days:
to be counted with the prisoners
(the last wish of the technically innocent)
in the Company of the wasted life
well-meanings for the conscience plate
or brief approval of the footlights' stare
and at noon, the windows burning our eyes.

First published in *Fire in the Afternoon*, Halstead Press 2014.

Swan Summers

By Dr. Kapardeli Eftichia

Swan summers
full of love
I lover of love
and mortal together

Cells of
beautiful trip
wounded by rose petals

A View From My Balcony

By Mary Anne Zammit

And so the sun with its golden light,
comes in with happiness.
Walking through the streets, warming my heart.
From long days in the shade.

The sun smiles,
casting its light.
Deep within my soul.
And August enters like crystals illuminating my balcony.

My soul rests there.
Embracing summer.

Let it be summer very day.
Let the sun shines on my balcony for all days to come.

The 'Cockpit Pews'
By John Tunaley

High noon, when an airman's neck cricks
As he constantly checks warrior sun.
I think of him as I look down at a
Small country populated with gravestones.

High June. Shadows strain to bury themselves
Under stiff stone-wall defenses weltered
In soared sorrel and alkanet bursts. Barbed
Bramble entanglements slash at the light.

A high moon, solstice full, will shine later
On a church closed before monumental
Masons made their killing. Where splayed bibles
Signal in vain to an intent blind world.

The world. A place laid waste and desolate.
One that conceives chaff and brings forth stubble.

Summer Breeze

By Pamela Scott

I wait for you by the open window
the summer breeze blows through my hair,
the suitcase sits on the floor beside me
and my lover sleeps in the darkness behind me.

I hear footsteps crunch on the gravel outside.
You've kept your promise after all.
I grab the suitcase and run downstairs
and barely glance at what I'm leaving behind.

I step out of my prison and into your arms.
The summer breeze whips around us.
I know I'm safe in your arms
and you won't let him hurt me again.

I press my face against your chest
as your safe scent surrounds me.
Your strong arms encircle me.
You whisper your love in my ear.

You carry my suitcase to your waiting car
and we chat about the places we'll go.
You take my hand and help me into the car.
I've left hell behind forever.

Summer

By Lynette Cupido

The season of warmth and love,
Where the sun light strokes the pain of cold
And lost love away.
Where you can feel the ray of light from God's
Love on your face and soul,
Being penetrated by warmth and love.
The season of everything being green and beautiful,
All the different blessings we were granted,
And ones taker for granted.
The warmth of the love we
Receive from family, friends and that
Someone special.
Especially God's love for his people.
The blue sky that smiles down on us.
Summer is a time to be outside,
Going to places visiting friends,
Watching the sunrise with
Someone special, and God
Watching over you.
Summer, the season of warmth and love.

The Tamworth Country Music Festival

By Mavis Atha
February 3rd 2015

Visitors camping
Sun is rising
Birds are singing
Leaves gently fluttering
Dogs begin barking
Folks already waking
and breakfast making
Peel street exciting
Buskers start playing,
competing, composing,
Fiddling, banjo-ing.
Jeans and hats wearing
Boots for line-dancing.
Then the Grand Opening
Crowds all picnicking
Bringing their seating
Everyone's eating,
Kasey Chambers entertaining
Country music playing
Crowds are all cheering
Sun is now setting
The day is now ending
Fireworks exploding.

The Moon Daughter's Garden

By Linda M. Crate

I am a daughter of the moon
wanting peace and kindness
solitude and silence
to the company of others
lost in nature's calming grace
and my elements are fire and water;
in the traditional zodiac I am a cancer
but in the Chinese I am a fire tiger
i can be both -
sometimes I am a calm wave others a fierce hurricane
I can be a well watched lit candle or a forest fire
but I prefer to be the sunlight of summer
falling down and kissing flowers
dancing upon streams and creeks
laughing through the arms and backs of trees
falling merrily and gracefully
through blinds
listening to birdsong pirouetting through the land -
I would rather be kind and soft
but sometimes there must be wars and so I send
hurricanes of erosion and flames of fury
when I must be tried;
but mostly I am the quiet daughter of summer
simply observing, living, dreaming
quaintly from my own garden

One Calm Morning

By Beaton Galafa

I walked up the 14th Avenue
whizzed with an aroma in the air
they breathe as they spit from the pavement
when the sun is tender and fresh.
I stood on a path to the hills
at the foot, marvelling at the tower
of gold in the jungles.
to welcome the sun as it rises,
wave a goodbye when night reigns.
Birds hummed into my ear from a distance
- that my friend, they call taxes.
For the sweat and blood, your brother comes -
as they lay on beaches with love and kisses from the sun
water bubbling to make the scenery even beautiful.
On trails, ants threw around mandibles
plundering and storing for generations,
no chief, no mansions, no tax.
Just a tower hiding their love from a midday sun,
As I remembered home.
That when the sun is low
dressing us in swarthiness at dusk,
babies go out, stare at the empty sky
waiting, for stars to fill hollowness
carved by grief.

Summers In Anstruther

By Pamela Scott

A narrow street leads
down from the holiday
chalet to a little shop
at the foot of the hill.

Every morning my
parents lead me down
it, while I tug the
lead of the family dog.

A narrow alley beside
the shop leads to
a secluded beach.

Early in the morning
we're the only ones there.

The sea breeze blows
in our faces, making our
hair wild, untamed.

I love the smell of
the sea and the sound
of the gulls, circling,
crying overhead.

I let the dog off
the lead. He runs
up and down the
beach, barking at
the waves.

Mum and Dad
sit on a little
stone bench.

I take off my shoes
and walk across the
sand to the edge of the
sea. The sand's warm
even at this early hour.

I stand where the sea
and sand meet, staring
out at the sea that goes
on forever, already
feeling my childhood
moving further into the past.

Four Views Of An Australian Summer

By Don Adams

Australia! The Great red Land, the place where I was born.
Exploring it confirms my love when summer's under way.
The Top End and the endless plains, the mountains, beaches they,
in warmer months, will follow patterns centuries have worn...

The dappled light part lifts the gloom where vicious vines array
tenacious tendrils armed with spurs and flesh are hard to hide.
Above me, from some hidden perch, indignant parrots chide
me for my trespasses, a pompous raucous roundelay.

I glance up at the canopy where leafy treetops ride
a gentle breeze. But here below no zephyr fans my face.
A whirl of bright-winged butterflies enchant me as they chase
Around me flaunting vibrant colours as they flit and glide.

They offer light relief from heat which casts its moist embrace
To black my mood. The sight of orchids lightens it instead.
Those floral gems of nature speckle tree trunks just ahead.
The 'spice of life' is all around this so contrary place.

The Cape in summer! Harsh and humid. Creatures that we dread!
There's beauty too and where you find it gold outweighs the lead.

~

I slit my eyes to cut the glare and peer across the plains.
They stretch towards infinity and there, the whole world long,
mirages tease to lure the lost. The devil's billabong.
An ancient land now roasted red through want of soaking rains.

Those hazy far horizons; through a light both harsh and strong,
support a skyline bleached a blue remorseless heat has made.
The soil is parched, a crumbling crust. Of grass there's not a blade.
And yet these plains are worshipped in our poetry and song!

In contrast, rains arriving bring cool beauty on parade.
The lush green grass is flecked with flowers, fresh from nature's
loom.
At present, though, the earth is swept by drought's dry dusty broom.

The ruthless sun burns out the air. We bless the river's shade.

Relentless heat and rainless years. A place resigned to doom.
Yet let the storms clouds gather. Then the plains will breathe and
bloom.

~

The rampant ranges! All around me, verdant, daunting, wild.
These rolling vistas spread afar to test the keenest sight.
With thrilling views and crisp sweet air the world is sheer delight.
In contrast to the western plains the summer days are mild.

Below me, in the gorges, with their shadows black as night,
the bell-birds' notes are ringing, singing, tinging crystal clear.
A magpie carols counterpoint and then, from somewhere near,
a flock of parrots flash on by in iridescent flight.

A merry gurgling rushing sound. A mountain stream I hear
cavorting through a dark ravine where cliffs, in cold disdain,
throw back my shouts to echo in a multi-voiced refrain.
The sounds of birds, of stream and bush! Delight to any ear.

You seek an ancient, untouched land? Then this is your domain.
The red rock pillars, soaring bluffs and greenswept vast terrain.

~

I walk along warm golden sands beside a blue-rinsed sea.
The waves are lapping idly in a gently swishing rip.
Above me, in a whirling cluster, seagulls flap and flip.
All starving by the sound of each beseeching, screeching plea.

Along the far horizon steams a dinky toy, a ship.
Its silhouette stands out against a pale celestial hue.
While carving out a foam-flecked path to reach a deeper blue
are sun-tanned swimmers. Through the swell I see them lift and dip.

The weather's hot. December hot, and worshippers pursue
obeisance to the sun gods while the children slip and slide
along the shallows, splashing, screaming. Bodies far and wide
are relishing the summer while the weather's warm and true.

A carefree time when troubles have been gladly cast aside.
Reality will set in soon, as will the coming tide.

~

I gaze across this great red land and feel a rush of pride
that grips me for Australia, from coast to way out back.
When I trudge off to Heaven let me walk an Aussie track.
And summer is the season I would have the fates provide.

AUTUMN

Still There

By Jasmine Kang

The sun rises,
shines and sets.
You might not see it
during a cloudy day,
but it is still there.
The light is still there.

You do not see stars in the daytime,
but they are still there.
The flower might fade,
but the winds carry its fragrance far,
and its sweet song is forever
remembered in our hearts.

The leaves might not be green
or part of the tree,
but that doesn't mean that's the end.
This is just the start
of a new beginning,
a new journey.

Like tiny bubbles
on the sea,
we come and we go
meeting and parting
like waves of the Ocean
destined to return Home.

Harvest Festival

By Tracy Davidson

harvest festival
she saves the biggest veggies
for the soup kitchen

Similar But Different: A Nostalgic Morning Reflection

By Mary Coons

As I relax in my second floor, freshly-decorated-for-Fall sitting room with an outdated home magazine and cooled off cup of coffee, my eyes are drawn across the small room to the screened patio and balcony; perfect size for my two tired lawn chairs and small side table that have sat vacant all summer and fall.

The late morning sun is sectioning off the space. Drifting in are the unmistakable smells of garlic and unknown spices that a resourceful cook somewhere in the area is adding, I suspect, to a pot of soup for someone's lunch.

The weather is gorgeous. It's still warm; 80 degrees in mid-November, with dirty sand and fine particles of dust clogging my nostrils, but then, this is the Middle East, and this Midwesterner from the U.S. has had three years to adapt to the climate. After all, just three weeks ago it hovered around 100 degrees - and back home it was snowing - so I consider myself lucky. It is what it is. I won't complain.

An occasional bird's song breaks the outside silence punctuated by a rumbling vehicle off in the distance.

Without warning, the many mosques in the neighborhood break out into sound; one of six daily calls to prayer. The male voices collide with one another via loudspeakers mounted high on minarets as they summon faithful Muslims to Zuhr, the noon prayer. Within three to four minutes, all is silent once again.

It's peaceful and calming. Comfy within my nondescript beige-walled compound, my mind wanders while my senses explode. My sense of smell is updating the garlic scent to suggest chicken soup with this distinct spice liberally added.

In moments such as this, I wonder about - and miss - my comfortable house back home; an old Victorian in a small rural town. It, too, welcoming the late morning aromas from the restaurant on the corner preparing for its lunchtime patrons, the many chirping birds, cars across the river slowly winding their way into town as they cross the bridge, and the daily noon whistle - once alerting the farmers in the fields of lunch time - now a time-honoured tradition sounding twice a day from the fire station two streets away.

The distance between here and there may be enormous, but in many respects, the daily routines are similar. Yes, there are differences; cultural, political, religious and social, but then 'different' is a good thing in my book.

Marmalade Moon

By Terry Hickland

A thousand mill on fireflies light up the Milky Way. The crescent moon slowly rises, slim and orange as a shred of marmalade, bathing the lonely field in a golden sheen.

Badgers timidly leave their den and drink in the evening air. A distant beat of wings draws ever nearer. Wild geese pass overhead, travelling to some far-flung place.

An old tawny owl perches high in a beech tree, its piercing eyes like lasers cutting through the night. Nocturnal life forms scurry back and forth in the undergrowth below.

Time, balanced on the earth's axis, ushers the night into dawn's arms, ready to begin another new day.

Winter Down Under

By Jennifer Riggs

No season of mists and fallow frightfulness,
No seasonal eclipse of outdoor fun,
No month on month of slow distress,
Of squall and sleet and squeamish sun;
No leaf-bare twigs on skeleton trees –
We're evergreen and ever bright:
Wattles, bottlebrushes, gums,
Blossoms, butterflies, sunlight.
Here only fridges wheeze and freeze –
For here, indeed, warm days will never cease.
We are in Queensland, where winter never comes.

November

By Mantz Yorke

As I read your words

winter's harbinger
is etching in snow
the secret furrows
where streams once echoed
the carelessness of love.

Shivering alders,
summer's conspirators
in intimacy, stand naked,
their twigs a filigree
against brindled hills.

Icy gusts
lash the beeches;
russet leaves
are tumbling down –
the dying fall

of remembrance.

A Walk Through These Empty Rooms

By Abigail George

Look, it is autumn. Autumn
rain. It is the beginning of a
brave new world. You don't
understand me. You love me,
you say you do, but you don't
understand me. I know of psychiatrists,
illness. Disability. I know of
medicine. Blood and water.
Cold flesh. 'Just go black,'
my mother says. It is fasting
time. Lightning and thunder in my body.
I always have to wait for the
tiredness to lift to do anything of importance.
The autumn chill is in the air.
The breakfast wasteland of it all.
Things of bittersweet regret.

The tap roots are enormous.
I knew a boy called Julian once.
He played the guitar. I wonder
what he is doing now. The girls
that he dances with. The girls
that he kisses. The heavens opened up. How to forget.
Bees and mist dance on the surface
of the earth. Darkness is lifted. Granite is trapped there.
The same way that case studies
are trapped in caves in high care.
Instinct tells me that I can't touch
love. That I can't touch the sun.
Branches have the autumn chill inside them still.
This is a post-apartheid river. The people here are lonely and sad.
Precocious and intellectual. In

a land faraway, people are
on the move. They are getting
out of bed. Waking their children, taking showers,
fixing breakfasts, fixing their hair.
I am so attuned to it now. Drinking
my coffee to birdsong. It is morning and sanctuary

is no more for now. 'Please love me,'
I said in my youth and my twenties.
Now I am saying, 'don't forget me.'

To Be Remembered Like Autumn

By Linda M. Crate

when the leaves sing
in beautiful shades of
emerald, canary, mulberry,
scarlet, carnelian, topaz,
and every shade beyond and between
my heart feels a certain sort of
happiness
because there is such beauty to be
found in the humble kiss of the wood;
I feel like exploring
the autumn flowers and see all the
beautiful trees
dressed in their best and brightest colours
taking me into a world that is far from the dark reality
media tries to paint for us because my
world is a lot kinder than
theirs -
in the heartbeat of autumn it seems
a miracle that I should be given such beauty
witnessing this magic when I am just a mere heartbeat
of all the heartbeats in this world,
and I hope that I remembered
fondly like autumn and all her beautiful array of colours
dancing in a ballet that comes
every year.

Faces Of Autumn

By David Watt

In turn leaves lower flushed and weary face,
Selecting perfect time and perfect place
To flutter way to ground as they must do,
Now summer's gone and stronger winds ensue;

Revealing in the process limbs of trees,
Reminding us that Life with gentle ease
Attains its zenith, has no choice but run
Right back to where its journey had begun.

And having made their blanket light and soft,
Leaves rustle as the autumn breezes waft,
Making music though they sleep unknowing;
Through the sun, the rain, each gust come blowing.

Awaken though they must each morning new
As children take delight in wading through,
And dogs nudge underneath, nose down, tail up,
Reliving lost exc tement as a pup;

And when the autumn days have run their course,
Leaves commenced decay with no recourse;
Reminisce the vibrancy of colour
Compared to coming winter's icy pallor.

Elegy For Autumn

By Barbara E. Robinson

I see autumn in it's waning days
when trees, unclothed, look quite forlorn.
Fallen leaves withered and early dawn
so bare of face, no chorus now
of pert blackbird or warbling thrush,
only the hush of deep, deep silence
and echoes of dreams forever lost.
Corn stubble fields and November mists,
unheathered moors and hedgerows bare,
the dying year is everywhere.

Is this the place that stirred my heart,
that is now stark, a cold closed door?
And I could weep for all that beauty,
the youthful days that are no more.
And would it not have been more kind
to dull my memories of this barren time
so I may live without sad dreaming,
no more that deep ache in my heart,
no more to mourn this desolation.

First published in *Free XpresSion* magazine, Australia

Autumn

By Bernadette Perez

listen whispers wind
whistling rattles current
harmony in sync

inhale autumn bliss
woe thy delicate flower
engage in purpose

life circle begins
fertilized with nutrients
searching for detail

leaves transcend to fall
harvest gathers fruitful crops
replenished by rain

dance through poppy fields
a symphony of pattern
composed progression

On Hearing The Smacks In Dark Autumn Lane

By John Karl Stokes
Coming down from The Pilgrims' Way

How green was my village then
when last I heard that last eleven:
the poets' white ghosts a-lurking
light verse falling at the Surrey end.

~

There is Yeats, beyond Ben Bulben
There Keats, outcast, out far
There Lawson, long legs a-dangling
and Banjo with his small guitar.
And young Les sitting on the wicket
The gasometer sinking in fading light
"There's more to life than cricket", says he,
The darling birds are taking fright.

~

But where are they now, the Boakes of the outfield,
out where the dead men fall
when Auden bowled the wrong'un
and Shaw Neilson caught it gentle?
Gone, all gone, with cattle.
The bagman plods his weary way.
None left to mourn, none left a-sobbing
The misty cries ascend the lea.

~

Now the Black Swan of Avon's had his way
with young Miss Hunter-Dunn
and Betjeman bowls the last, last,
maiden... and quiet, flows the Don.

First published in *Cricket Poems*, 2001.

Autumn: The Season Of Love

By Sourabh Acharya

As the season of love arrives so soon
Cynosure of the nights deludes the moon

For the love of the rhyme
And some of that, of the freezed time
I crave for the falling leaves before monsoon
Maybe for the seasonal colour of maroon
Or for the dalliance of the sun and noon
The trees commit a beautifully dulcet crime
As the season of love arrives.

For nature is what gifts us this boon
Entangles us w thin its silenced tune
Some more halcyony of the musical sublime
Emollient glamour of the falling prime
Rises up above the glad grinning balloon
As the season of love arrives.

Grey Curls

By Terry Hickland

Light grey curls of smoke rise like a spirit leaving this earth, becoming lost in a clear blue morning sky.

Beech leaves, sap drained from their short lives, crackle and hiss above the reddened embers. A rake's worn hooks corral the leaves autumn has left behind into an uneven pile.

The old man, walnut pipe balanced on withered lips, works at a languid pace, his prey fallen around him like the mighty Chinese Terracotta Army.

A mellow breeze comes to make mischief, its breath chasing a few dry leaves on their way.

Their shrivelled bodies toss and tumble, scraping along the cobbled pathway like the tiny claws of mice scuttling under floorboards as winter draws near.

Buttermere, October

By Mantz Yorke

Gloom. Grubby wool softly shearing
the Buttermere crags, and the path
to High Stile merely a radius
of circumscribed perception: no prospect
for the camera but the muddy track
and grasses seeded with mist. We descend

a glaciated scour, with no expectation
the sun will break the cloud to rouse
yellowing leaves to a vivid valediction
from spiky branches rendered black.
You tell me yet again to live the present,
not frustrated possibility, and to find delight

in muted hues – the purplish haze
suffusing trees whose sepia trunks
are randomly daubed with lichen's green,
and the lakeside larches' knobbly tan
trailing across the slaty reflection
of Fleetwith Pike. Yet when we return

from transgressing boundaries
to dreary days of domesticity and work,
there'll be no photographic print,
no footmarks fossilised in mud,
no pencilled sketch, nothing
but traces on the palimpsest of mind.

Falling Leaf

By Kirsty A. Niven

Free-falling towards the earth,
your safety chord cut.
Edges crumbling into the crisp air,
becoming one with dust.
You plummet like the apples
before you,
landing with a moist squish.
The season is over.

Autumn

By Brian Langley

Now autumn is the time for picking apples
That have grown on the trees all summer long
And autumn is the time for April showers
And when Easter time and ANZAC come along

In autumn, many leaves turn brown and wither
And fall upon the footpaths of our town
Making them all slipp-ery to walk on
So be very careful that you don't fall down

And autumn is the time for chilly mornings
And getting colds that make us cough and sneeze
Its also when our government quite often
Increases many charges, tax and fees

Now I'm not keen on apples, I love strawberries
And rain makes fallen leaves all 'yuck' with slime
And I don't need additional expenses
Oh! - If only I could bring back summer time

Pew 26

By John Tunaley

Beethoven has died away, his music
Has dissolved into plaster and stonework.
At sub-atomic levels you can hear
His late quartets; submerged and distorted.

Ludwig found out just how deaf he was at
St Stephen's in Vienna. Twenty-three
Bells rang, he heard nothing but saw startled
Birds fly from the cathedral belfry.

The gold fields that were cut off at the knee
Already have their complexions greying.
In this open weather, the gouging plough
Is half obscured by clouds of silent gulls.

I've missed the concert, for this is the wrong church,
Still I'm sat in this pew and listening hard.

17/09/2014, Old St Stephen Church, Robin Hood's Bay

A Woman Must Always Keep A Journal

By Abigail George

I watch the fragments of
the sun in the history of water.
Agriculture reminds me
that nothing dies a natural death.

Little birds build the world they want with despair.
They are as thirsty as my universe is. Everything

is bleak here. Made of hardship.
Solitude and loneliness.
Man, wake up your soul on this Sunday morning!
You're a collection of essays.
Hope and suffering. The blues.
A country made of coconut
milk and ice cream. Autumn.

There is blessing, nature, the
maturity of meat in your voice.
We have both been getting on
in years. Two aunts walked
down the aisle. Farewell Atlantis.
You're a beautiful stranger to me now.
Even the moths want to be

accommodated now in this
post-apartheid South Africa.
There is a music school behind his
wet stone eyes. Aspects of love.
This is why the sea does not
glitter anymore during the day.
I was happy once when I was

connected to you. When you
held me in your arms and kissed me.
There when I found the sun.
The sky was ancient there until
I came upon the sun. The moon-
light had no melody or chords.
It was raining men and women and

when the radiant sun came out

it rained golden. I came to life in her tiny kitchen in Cape Town.

I was the polite and fragile one.
I used her steaming pots and
clay face mask. Her bath oils
and her umbrella. Her flat was near
the mountain. I would drink
her tea all by myself in the afternoons
before she came home from work. She belonged
to the autumn asphalt jungle.

Autumn

By Rebecca Sutton

The leaves falling on the highway
and the trees are starting to grow old.
With the icy wind beginning to blow through my face,
the land now inhabits another time, another place.

With a land of sepia-like green,
something that I always like to see.
The cows walking their own way,
and the sheep pulling their blankets down.

Autumn always signals the end,
the end of long summer days
and nights that seem to go on and on.
Yes there is always a sadness there,
but also a hope.

A hope that summer will come again,
after a long, embracing winter.

Flowers Aren't Always Restful To Look At

By Kirsty A. Niven

You survive everywhere – parasitic, feeding from others.
It's the only way for you, roaming and subsisting.

Compared to you, they are so unblemished;
their pomaceous handfuls so fresh and untouched.

Fairly inconspicuous, your ivory petals overripe.
They look right through you. I should too I suppose.

All fluorescence is fading, both of you losing colour.
I know you are perishing. That's how it always works.

Once autumn's finished, they always wither and die.
Everything dehydrates; one last splurge then nothing.

Home disappears and white death is all that's left.
The fires are beginning; the dried remains so easily inflamed.

The strips of petal curl and twist in the flames.
Their delicate silhouettes scattering in the breeze.

You used to be striking. You were overly vivid.
Too full of life, overbearing to the dull of my eyes.

Now I regret my hatred of you,
as it is now barren

because you left.

Winter Is Approaching

By Olivia Matthews

On this frosty morning I feel the temperature plummet.
As I step outside my face feels the crisp morning air.
My breath turns to foggy mist, floating on the gentle breeze.
My face squeals in shock as a frosty wave progresses over it.
My head shies away from the cold, under its warm woollen nest.
My body feels relief under its many smothering layers.
My nose won't cease running until it reaches warmth.
My fingers near the brink of complete and utter numbness as they
slowly turn beet-red.
My toes nestle further down into my sheepskin lined boots.
I snap on the camera to get a vivid picture of autumn.
Winter is approaching...

WINTER

Christmas Eve
By Tracy Davidson

Every year the same old story,
rushing around on Christmas Eve.
Though Santa still gets all the glory,
every year the same old story.
Finding Nemo, Finding Dory,
another sack of goods to heave.
Every year the same old story,
rushing around on Christmas Eve.

Winter's Fuel

By Terry Hickland

Bare soles tread the frosted meadow, grass collapsing underfoot as fine crystal. The girl's brown petticoat hem, once white as elderflower, trails reluctantly behind.

Rays of sunlight form a golden stairway through the murky greyness. Curlews cuss and make a din, hidden by swirling mist that moves without purpose.

A young body, taut as a fiddler's bow, begins its task. Unkempt, raven-black hair brushes the darkened earth as she stoops to pack the bricks of turf into a frayed basket of hazel.

Calloused hands are plunged into an ice cold spring. Droplets of water cascade over chapped lips, becoming needles of fire. A worn Claddagh brooch secures her tattered shawl.

Aged leather straps creak in protest as the basket is drawn to her back. A donkey comes into view, such a civil beast, idly awaiting its burden.

The pair will ply the worn trail with winter fuel until the old, dry-stone byre can hold no more.

Christmas In July

By Mavis Atha

It's time to think mulled port and kippers
Warm fireside and cosy slippers
Baked dinner, stuffing, cranberry sauce,
Christmas pudding, another course
Finish with, just for old time's sake
A slice of cheese and Christmas cake.

We'll pull our crackers, tell our jokes,
It's good to laugh with all our folks,
Then 'pass the parcel', 'the minister's cat',
Watch 'A Christmas Carol', plus chocolate,
Sing a carol, share a tale,
Have a beer, a wine, or ginger ale.

Candles flicker with their warming glow,
Christmas tree with star for us to know,
Looking on the floor around the tree
Token gifts for you and me,
The reason we celebrate and why,
We have Christmas in July.

Cumbrian Winter

By Kathleen Boyle

Getting through another winter,
bone cold, damp lunged,
They trim the tree and stick bright snowmen
To frosted glass,
While on a rain-soaked
Cumbrian landscape,
Sheep bleat in the dark.
Cosy indoors,
Christmas is underway.

Winter

By Clare Lightfoot

Time passed night fell
No distinction between day and night.
Darkness hung like a shroud around the village.

The snow was heavy
Rutted lanes were blocked.
Life was contained
In the cottages.

People slept huddled together.
All the families in one bed
For warmth.
The children curled
Around each other like kittens.

Daybreak without cocks crow?
The hens and cocks huddled together
For warmth.
Nothing stirred.

A watery sun was lost in the heavy clouds.
It was day but felt like night.

They broke the ice in
The basin to wash
Dressing hurriedly against the cold.
Pulling on damp clothes
As the cold seeped into their bones.

The mother rubbed
The children's feet.
Pulling onto tight cold toes
Socks with holes in them.
She tucked the holes under their toes.
Pushing their feet into boots too large
Without soles.

At least it was
Some protection
Against the cold.

A scramble for sweaters
Ensued
Old and raggy
They offered little warmth.
Everyone soon had a sweater.
Oversized too big
Tied around them.

The peat fire was lit
To boil water for porridge.
The cottage filled with acrid smoke.
Making the little ones cry and gasp!

The chimney was blocked
With snow.
The father tried to open the door?
It was blocked

He climbed out through
A window.
Shouting for the elder boys to help.
Soon snow was being pushed away from the door.

Smoke spewed outside
As the door inched open.
The father climbed
On the roof
Released the snow.

The makeshift chimney
Sucked at the
Peat smoke like a dying man.
Life was hard.

Meagre porridge made
More water than oats
But it was hot
The family were thankful.

Slowly the cottage
Began to warm.
The loom was set.
The woman began to weave.

The cottage was suddenly buzzing.

The click of the shuttle
Was a soothing noise.
Thread was woven into cloth.

The children carded
The wool between spiked blocks.
The husband
Separated the wool from its bails.
The older boys
Helped him.

The big stone sink was filled with hot water.
The wool was washed
And pummelled by hand.
Home-made soap to
Clean it.

The man's hands
Were cracked and sore.
He packed the cloth.

Hoping to make
The perilous trek
To the market.
Praying for his feet
To hold steady.

Desperate for the
Few pennies
To feed his ever
Growing brood.

His wife mopped her brow,
Her belly swollen against
The loom.
This baby
Would not wait till the spring.
Her time was soon.

Eight pairs of hungry eyes looked
At her.
She was overcome
With sadness
At the stark reality.

Ice formed patterns
On the inside of the windows.
They began to melt
Making the cottage
Damp.

Surely this awful weather
Would go.

The father left
He would be gone
Three days.
He took the elder boys
Maybe they would
Find a rabbit for stew.

Night settled
Snow fell
The cottage once again
Cold and dark.

The last candle spent.
The mother mustered
Her energy.
Boiled water
Used the last of the meal.
Fed the children.
Not herself.

Long days passed
The children
cried
With hunger.
The husband did not return.

the mother prayed
For the lord
To take them.

The villagers
Found them in the spring
Huddled together like kittens.

Time passed night fell
No distinction between day and night.

All-Season

By Brigette Furlonger

Lambs wool filled duvet for all seasons. Well, at least that's what the duvet package said. Enclosed in plastic, it was difficult to know if it was possible. Rebecca had yet to experience such a thing. Something that could weather all seasons.

Sleeping was a problem in a home with no climate control. And with any control of her climate, she experienced each season acutely. Summertime meant doing away with any covers other than a light sheet, but she had often woken up cold. Rebecca would yank the covers over herself only to push them off within the hour. It had never been great, but it was manageable.

Now, in the winter, it was always cold getting into bed. Rebecca would wear pyjamas that went from her neck to her ankles, and sometimes she even wore socks. But by two in the morning she was suffocating. Piled with blankets, she still couldn't get warm, but also, couldn't breathe. Stuck in bed, she would remain much too long considering spring, summer and autumn.

Rebecca longed for spring that held a cool breeze that promised warmth. The scent of the flowers, the buds and the beginnings felt like a lifetime away. When the leaves had begun to turn, it felt like the world said 'look at magnificent me'. In late autumn the russet leaves crackled, then fractured and had since been swept away.

"How much for the duvet?" Rebecca asked the sales woman.

"Six hundred and ninety-nine dollars." The woman smiled with her straight white teeth. "It'll last you a lifetime."

"Can I get a guarantee for that?"

"Absolutely," the woman said without hesitation.

"Good." Rebecca grinned, keeping her thin lips over her stained dentures. "It's for my great granddaughter."

The sales woman blinked, smile gone.

Snow In Winter

By John R. Sabine

Of course we get snow in winter in Australia. Even though Australia is regarded as the direst continent, we still get loads of the stuff, spread particularly all over our mountains in the south east. We even call them the Snowy Mountains, though by European or American standards I suppose Snowy Hills might be more appropriate. Indeed, in terms of area alone, our snowfields cover more than the whole of Switzerland.

There is a big difference, however, between our snow and that of most of the rest of the world. We can take it or leave it. Well, most of us can. Let me explain.

The vast majority of Australians live in our big cities. Those cities in the South-East - Sydney, Melbourne, Adelaide, Hobart, Canberra even, which is at a higher altitude (not quite 600m) than the rest, which are all coastal – where you might expect winter snow, generally receive the merest dusting on surrounding hills perhaps one in five or ten years. Most of it lasts less than 24 hours. Thus, if you want to see snow, you have to go further afield to find it. And then you can leave it and go back home, even in the depths of winter.

As a kic growing up in Melbourne I had "been to the snow" probably no more than three or four times. Most likely to Mount Donna Buang (1,250m), some 80km from the city. And of course really only to play in it.

Consequently I had never met real snow until, in my mid-twenties, I went to the American Mid-West, the University of Illinois at Champaign/Urbana. I arrived around September 1, but of course it wasn't until several months later that we had our first snowfall. I vividly remember walking across campus early that morning just as it began snowing. I was fascinated. Enjoyed it immensely. Stuck my tongue out to catch the flakes, gathered some for a snowball or two, all that sort of kid stuff.

All of course to the great amusement and/or horror of anyone seeing me. What an idiot, I am sure, would have been the general consensus. As you might expect, however, after I had been there for the best part of three years and had experienced a few decent snowfalls and a couple of ice-storms I was not so enamoured. I still preferred to go to the snow, rather than have it come to me.

But, as many Americans and most Canadians will rightly tell me, central Illincis is hardly snow country. Ok, then, I did try to walk around a snowy down-town Chicago when the temperature was minus two degrees, and didn't enjoy the experience. My real awakening, however, came some years later when I was invited to the University of Iowa, Iowa City, one mid-January. Just walking the hundred yards or so from the parking garage to the lab building was an experience I can cheerfully leave to others. Maybe it was only minus 15 or so, but there was also something that I had barely heard of before, let alone experienced. The 'chill factor.' I certainly now know what it means. And you can keep it.

My real snow education, however, came when I set out to return home. Not sure now where home was at the time, but clearly somewhere nicer and warmer. Or at least without any chill factor. My host prepared to take me to the airport, barely twenty miles of so down the relevant Interstate. But I felt as though we were preparing for a trans-arctic expedition – shovel, sandbags, extra blankets, some sort of portable heater I think, a companion to accompany him on the way back from the airport. For just twenty miles on a major highway! Simply par for the course, I was told.

Snow? If I want to see some I'll go and find it. You can keep the rest.

Winter Morning, Cold Snap

By Pamela Scott

Another inch of snow fell during the night
burying the rest of the street in white.
Cold everywhere, I can't seem to get a heat in me,
don't know when this cold snap will finally end.

Everything looks to beautiful and pure indoors,
Fresh snow, untouched and undisturbed –
great for walking on. I love footprints in the snow.
Hellish when you need to go further than the end of the street.

I breathe and leave a white mist on the ice cold windows.
Just wish I didn't have to leave the house. I could just stand here and watch.
Knock off my shift and pretend to be sick? Maybe I could say I'm snowed in and can't get out?
Love if I could just crawl back under the hot duvet and go to sleep.
Cosy and warm.

My hands feel like ice even though the heating is on, turned up full blast.
Never got on well with the winter. I like my comforts and being all snug and warm,
only crazy people love the snow and cold. I wish it was summer and melting heat.
Pang for sunshine, heat on my face, leaving the window open at night and ice cream.

Quiet mornings and it seems to be dark night and day. The sun died weeks ago.
Race to work and race home every day. If I slow down it feels like my bones are freezing.
Sometimes I wish I could hibernate in a hot place for four months a year.
Tea with two sugars and milks seems to thaw the ice inside me a little bit.

Under the weather seems to be my permanent mood during the winter.
Vacation in a hot place that's never seen the snow would be heaven right now.
Wish I could just escape to the sun and come back in time for June.

X-rated words spill from my mouth as soon as I step outside.

Yell in pain as the cold morning air touches my already ice-cold fingers.
Zero tolerance for snow and cold and ice. I hurry to work, head down.

Winter Solstice
By Mantz Yorke

December: charcoal scratches on an ash-grey page,
depression hanging nimbus over the beeches
and droplets on leafless branches.

Not like the last time I came here: then an encirclement of gold
and squirrels scrabbling in the fallen leaves, unaware
of the coming cold. No, merely a sodden landscape weeping
into mirrors, turning the world upside down. We dawdle
along the pathway, talking about pain

until, from the overcast, a slant of light hints
that we must leave this refuge, regain the main road
and soon return to those who'll never know
where we have been

Our slow walk slows and stops. Eyes meet, and soft lips
tenderly affirm a truth we'd never dared to say,
as tribal cerements crumble to the touch.
Our cold bones have waited, long-barrowed,
deep within the dark, till this midwinter sun should shine,
and we tremble as its late rays fall.

Daffodils At Christmas

By Chrys Salt

Gay as a blackbird's beak
your daffodils unbud
and burst into frilled trumpets
this Christmas morning,
bringing a torch of freshness
to the season's ritual,
reminding the heart's cold bulb
of its green, forgotten centre.
Better to have left the corner bare
than focus this bright beam
on the chill comfort I have grown to.
Better not to dare
this incandescent flame
for fear its clear and unexpected shining
blinds me into love,
and, sweeter then sap, your gentleness
enters my bones
calling my roots to draw up joy again.

Snowflake

By Kirsty A. Niven

In our cottage, echoing in silence,
words became taboo;
inducing an early winter.
The snow fell in hordes,
pitter-pattering
down upon the town.
We let go
of our silent vows,
as its flaking lullaby began.
With numb gloved fingers,
we moulded her,
sculpting the perfect doll
We glazed her porcelain skin with ice,
crudely poked in her eye sockets;
our own Frozen Charlotte.
We longed for her eyes to flutter open,
even for just one glassy glance.

The Land And Skies Of Mystery

By Clare Roslington

We walk slowly up the hill
In awe of the magic in the air today.
There is no breeze, just a gentle sweetness
Bathing us in peace.

The sun is shining,
But it is a subtle light
That warms and soothes our being,
And brightens colours and forms
Of leaves and berries.

As we walk higher,
We see the mists arising from the land
That soften the sounds,
Creating a womb-like atmosphere
Of mystery and serenity.

The land is submerged in mist
Yet silver green trees and fields can just be seen,
Soft and silent like sea plants, deep underwater.
On the far-off distant horizon, the mountain tops
Emerge from the white sea, like islands.

We gaze at the wide pastel skies
That paint ethereal peach pink hues
Around the setting sun.

All appears transformed into a new realm
That awakens the heart to deeper mystery
And wonder,
Creating space for a fresh vision;

A truer seeing
In just being with the mystery,
Not wishing the mists to clear
But welcoming them in
As part of oneself.

Winter

By Brian Langley

Our farmers sow their seeds of grain
when winter time is nigh.
It germinates and it grows tall
as winter passes by.

There's oats and rye, canola too
There's barley and there's wheat.
We watch them grow; the grains, they form,
Though yet they're incomplete.

In spring, these grains, they thicken up
till harvest comes along.
Then they become the food of life
that make us big and strong.

So that's why winter's special,
the best time of the year.
For that's the time the barley grows
And from barley, we make beer.

Fixing Winter

By Brian Langley

Winter time, I do not like; the days are much too short;
too dark for early rising, for surfing or for sport
and after work, the eve'nings, they're really much too dark
for catching fish or swimming, or jogging in the park.

The answer to this problem? It's very plain to see;
I'd have it fixed in no time, if it was up to me.
For as the UV index, in winter time is low,
that's the time to be outdoors, the time for us to go

down to the beach for fishing, or up on mountain peaks
skiing on the winter slopes, you could, for many weeks.
There's many days in winter, when these things could be done;
rain comes down just now and then, there's really lots of sun.

So how to fix up winter and make it fit to live
From May right through to August? My thoughts on it I'll give
The answer to this question, I'll tell you loud and clear:
All work should be forbidden, those four months of the year.

Wet Season: Flood On The Darling

By John Karl Stokes
A River in the Dark...

Speak now:
      seeing the words
sluiced, glistening,
a mouthing of breath,
redyellow
screeches;
green parrots
from eyelids

and dreams,
dreams, colouring
the whispers
of wings on
the flood lips:
the landbirds
wheeling into winter.

First published in *A River in the Dark*, Five Islands Press 2003.

When It's Cold

By S'busiso Manqa

If one remembers not
Who they are
In the cold,
They'll probably never.

When the breeze is soft
Yet pierces the skin,
And the masses scatter,
Selfishly yet rightfully
Behind closed doors
Without a helping hand to lend
Even to a friend next door.
Sadly this we learn,
Only you – you have to adore.

A season,
Where a farmer waters not,
Only to harvest
And feed his own –
Only to harvest
And feed his own.

In this season,
Days are never dark.
Only lonely
For those whom are not aware.

Wahoo!
By Madhavi Tiwary

I am a winter woman - not because I intend to bash other seasons, but because I wish to paint winter on these pages as a season worth making a masterpiece about.

Let me start with a recent international speech contest I witnessed. The on-the-spot topic given to the speakers was; "Winter is coming, how would you prepare?"

Well, a l speakers expectedly talked about winter as a time tough enough to be ready for. We all understand the undertones when we hear 'winter' as an allegory to the lows of life.

I always wonder, don't we prepare for celebrations too? For me, winter is a celebration – a celebration of all things cool and all things crazy.

I find smart winter woollens quite dependable comrades who dutifully camouflage my little tummy. You see, my little tummy has a rather sizeable social presence – only due to its curious temperament which makes it protrude whenever important people are around. However, winter invariably beats it at its 'unsocial' game by subtly imprisoning it under the pull over folds.

Other than the mega winter pay cheques like the one above, there are many small but noteworthy 'winter-wellness' examples. The gardens explode with colours of bountiful blooms. The mountain tops look saintly in their silver gowns of serene snow. All baby cheeks blush with deep crimson chills. Fragrance of the forest rides the air through the towns and the taverns. Most notably, the sun gleefully regains its popularity.

On a personal note, winter makes it a little easier for me to look at the overcrowded public buses in the financially less fortunate countries. My heart does not bleed as it does when the heat stricken human beings are swarmed together ruthlessly to get drenched in each other's sweat. The scenario changes pleasantly in winter. The same sea of humanity seems to be embracing each other - relishing the naturally extended warmth. They no longer look as dismal as they do in other seasons.

A sense of graciousness generally abounds. The uncontrollable shivers of the less fortunate in lean clothing, easily move the hearts of the more fortunate who have loads of snugly stuff to spare. A sense of sharing sneaks into even habitually closed hearts.

I cherish my travels in winter and I relish my stories of winter. The few hugs that I get, linger longer in winter. For some intriguing reason, I have made many more friends in winter than in any other season. Little episodes that happened because of winter have enriched my memories. My car cleaner about a dozen years back still surprises me with his calls just to say hi and that he misses me – only because on one windy, wintry day I had impulsively gifted him my woollen scarf. I don't think any other season would have prompted me to indulge in that tiny action that won me an admirer for life.

I earnestly advocate winter as the season of most comforting warmth. Knitting sweaters for the loved ones still counts as one of the most emotionally stirring activity. A simple but steaming cup of tea is still one of the highest bonding factors among human beings. Cuddling on the pretext of avoiding the chill, still remains one of the supremely savouring signals of romance.

O magical winter, please keep me under your spell forever!

Winter Fishing

By David Watt

On a foggy winter's morning we put our boat to sea,
Fully laden with provisions, Uncle Pat, the dog, and me.
The fish large and ferocious, we reeled in with great delight –
By sunset, tired, contented, we soon settled for the night.

Early in the morning we awoke to different scene
Of wind almost cyclonic, seas no longer flat, serene.
The cabin radio through static declared as if to mock:
"A winter storm approaching! Fishing boats return to dock!"

So we set our sails for homeward (more figurative than true) -
As smoky diesel motor pushed us up, and down, then through;
And Pat turned sort of greenish, while dog barfed, too ill to bark.
As for me? Well I felt awful, like a fire lacking spark.

Eventually we made it back to dock and solid ground,
Which we kissed in gratitude, or slobbered thanks like hound!
When feeling slightly better, we together made a pact -
In future, winter fishing would be grounded, lightly-packed!

Stream Of Thought

By Barbara E. Robinson

At dawn I walk the old worn track
that rounds the hills where paths diverge
and there I tread the higher trail
to gaze down on a frozen stream.
Its stillness echoes ghostly carols,
no clarity there nor leaf on bough.
Robed in ermine, snow on snow,
each tree stands tall with dignity.
Then flutters Blackbird from a branch,
sends crystal flakes to dance on air
and pirouette, waltz gently down
to peacefully rest on winter's lap.
Soon shafts of sun like fine spun gold
paint winter's snow a warmer shade of cold.
Did Ovid tread this land... but no...
If he had glimpsed this noble valley
he would have claimed it for his own,
a paradise to inspire a thousand poems.

Winner of the 'Winter' competition, *Salopeot* magazine

The First Of The Season

By Bernadette Perez

solace drifts calmly
deprived perception in a storm
waves convey farewell

vision from window
drops of rain descend music
ringing in the cold

pillows of powder
a blizzard violently blown
high winds straight ahead

cold temperatures drop
overwhelming is the view
stopped me in my tracks

follow me frozen
patterns will melt away change
transform within time

a transfer of heat
sought by the warmth of daylight
on a freezing day

light reflects pillows
exposed to all the elements
earth tilts dark to light

The Wind

By Mavis Atha

So you comb your hair, check your reflection's okay,
Leave the house to go shopping, start of a new day.

The fly screen door flies out of your hand
You nearly fall over from the step where you stand!

You climb in the car which shuts far too quick,
The bang on your leg makes you feel sick.

Bags fly round the ground when taking the waste
Then drive on to Aldi there's a feeling of haste.

For that's how you feel when it's windy outside
Restless, fractious and grumpy beside.

Blowing you here, blowing you there
Why did you both combing your hair?

Let's get back home and put on the TV
Have a hot cuppa and put a rug on my knee!

Sunlight And Winter

By David Watt

Winter do you hear me 'neath your veil
Of fine-spun silver shrouded icy pale?
Do you wonder why your nights are long
And the sun sh nes weaker, never strong?

Set your mind to thoughts of warmer days
When you hard y noticed Sunlight's rays;
Prompting coldness, as a woman scorned,
Resulting in a landscape frost-adorned.

Now her heart embittered chills to core
As punishment befitting notice poor;
Vivid in each gaze a deep offence,
Despite your shivered cries of innocence.

Though affection seems a hope forlorn,
Start again with praise for beauty borne
Of smile sure to win in any season,
Radiance surpassing wildest reason.

Then to emphasise your love is true,
Compliment her sparkle each day new;
Swear that simple "Aah!"s cannot convey
The miracle of coldness framed by ray;

And as your words successfully repair
Bridges to her heart rebuilt with care,
Take within your arms her precious light,
Sufficient for the season, subtle white.

Sunday Morning

By Mantz Yorke

Guttering cracks as the sun breaks
through the day's imprisoning grey.
Dark footprints mark my progress

across silvery grass, from grow-bags
of tomatoes that remain firmly green,
past the crab whose aromatic, waxy

midge-speckled fruits lie at random
after last night's storm, to a radiant
Gloire de Dijon among the weeds. Scents

of damp earth mingle as I fork out
couch and chickweed, readying the bed
for the winter months' neglect.

A sharp rattling of lids calls me
back to the kitchen: I lower the gas
beneath overboiling vegetables,

uncork the red wine (too late, as usual),
and baste again the crackling lamb
the un-breakfasted are dying to consume.

Winter's Night Awakening

By Clare Roslington

Stillness softening over the green fields
Grey clouds tinged orange by the setting sun
As the landscape is graced
By the air's cooling calm breath
Of the awakening mystical winter's night

A buzzard glides silently across the darkening wide skies
Two tiny birds that seem silver in this light fly home
Over bare limbed forest
To their welcoming cosy nest

Our breath becomes calm as day turns into night
Feeling the awakening of the gentle inner light
As we let go of the day's concerns
And allow nature to enter our hearts
And replenish us with truth

Fears and worries melt away
With the ending of the day
A song of love arises in the soul
As we come home to ourselves
Being present with no other goal

We are here
We are now
In this moment of grace
In nature's loving and comforting embrace

Worst Winter

By John Tunaley
El Invierno Lo Por

Madrid in time of civil war. Snow lies
On the burnt ground beneath a cold grey sky.
The incendiarists whirl their petrol
Bombs from home-made slings then they cling and loll
On skewed roofs. The dome of San Fernando
Starts to smoke. In the hills around Caso
Del Campo shellfire flashes from siege guns
That fill the air with sharp punctuation
And rolling thunder. Ticker tapes spit out
Rhetoric. Heroic figures strike stout
Picture poses. Each side fights for their true
History. The butchery continues
While at Paris' Grand Exposition
'Guernika' faces its Last Admission.

A Swirl Of Starlings

By Tracy Davidson

a swirl of starlings
reflected in frozen ponds
the sky their canvas

The Wind Beneath

By Courtney Speedy

he is the wind beneath
my skin and the rain
cloud over my heart
for he is proud yet I
am tearing us apart
like leaves from an
oak tree that winter
found too fast and
is begging for spring
to give him one last
chance.

Freezing Scout

By Beaton Galafa

I will rush to the tower and ring a bell.
When you strike at dawn,
You must not ambush the sun
Or send us down to spring out when the earth is still,
Lying on frost staring at the grey sky
Birds quietly humming from the cracking branches
Wondering if boots and cardigans can breathe into our mouths
A chilly spring from the mountain rocks.
We will hide in the whispers of wind
Blowing over the leaves gleaming in moonlight
Craving death that survives even hoar
Prances towards prey even in snow
To warm freezing heads and horns
As our blood clogs beneath the pores
Shrinking us where limbs meet the head
In a sickle that survives life.
As we live by hearths grinding teeth
Waiting for the garrisons to crack -like dawn and sun
We recount chronicles filled with rage and war, and
Lies. And hope to sterilize the young −even the old
From fear should you hunt us down:
With ice we wet throats moments before we die
As it melts when the orange sun strikes.
Yet we live for the horrors of another season.

Winter Blues

By Pamela Scott

It's cold today. There's no sun
or light in the sky. Everything's
wilting in the cold air
of winter. The trees are shrivelled
and blackening. The old world is dying.

My heart feels just
like the trees. My branches
are bare. I've wilted. I've got
no life or breath in me. My heart
is barely beating. I feel disconnected.

I can't seem to shake these
blues. The cold winter
air doesn't help. The cold fits
my gloomy mood. My
head feels to heavy to
hold up high. My spine
made of iron. I feel too heavy
for my frail body to
stand up straight.

I drag my leaden feet
through inches of crisp
white snow. I feel myself
getting slower every second.
It's like an invisible lead is
hauling me back. The
cold wind makes my
face ache.

My hands are like ice inside
heavy woollen gloves. My
fingers are tingling and sore.
I squeeze my numb hands
into my jacket pocket
and yearn for something
to give.

The Class Of Year 10

By John Tunaley

Near the un-manned crossing something heavy
Caught the herd of big-eyed deer by surprise.
Bewildered heads thrown back in agony
Muzzles bleeding, they died in disbelief...
Down at the river we'd turned at the point
Where snowy slush-capped waves threatened the dyke.
We lost Dad but at last found him, asleep
In a hedgerow ..anointed with frost...
Planing the land as flat as a butcher's block,
The ice flew in fast from Norway in the
South-east and from Shap Fell in the north-west.

It's trash collection day. The glacier
Makes no distinctions and given time will
Recycle all the blue, black and green bins;
Grinding them to paste in remorseless jaws...
It's taken out the town, hit the school gates
And lurks there...growling away to itself...
Huddled together for safety we
Take stock of the room. A plastic bag, half
Filled with hidden emotions, sits on the
Floor and gives nothing away. We've no knife,
So, tear our bread apart with trembling hands.
For most of us, even pointless scribbling
Proves an impossibly difficult task...

No-one can concentrate when any day
Our world may catastrophically end.
The ice may retreat...it may melt away,
But what else awaits us... just round the bend...?

Remembering You

By Rebecca Sutton
For Judith

I remember you.
Running on our own piece of land,
your legs kicking and bending in the air.
Your hair floating in the wind.

I remember you.
In the little church, with the red wooden door.
Your simple white dress
floating and magnifying against the sunlight.

I remember you.
With your children in the garden.
The barren trees as your signposts,
your clothes making signal in the air.

I remember you.
Sitting in your outdoor chair
watching the soft sunset, where the sun meets the clouds.
Your fingers wrapped around your personal chalice.

I always remember you
in our sun-filled winters.
Sun brightening the colours,
yet as chilly as your vintage ice-box.

Now you are gone
and I experience my sunny winters without you,
and no day is as wonderful
as that sunny, winters day I spent with you.

Within My Gardens Soul

By David Hollywood

Within my gardens soul abounds,
A spirit stirring neath the ground,
Aroused by secret depths that found,
Concealed, inspired, a place profound.

And as the rustling leaves surround,
With stories from the breezes sound
The haunting wind shall sing and pound,
Upon the life beneath this mound.

And in this knol of moistened dirt,
Where worms dig deep into the earth,
The tubers turn to sleep from hurt,
As winter storms its first alert.

And slumber waits for times delay,
To show how seasons laws obey,
Arousal's that deny decay.

Say What You See

By Tracy Davidson

Cloudwatching on a winter's day...

I see a pod of dolphins
racing each other across the sky.

I see a rearing horse
that, just for a moment,
thanks to a passing plane's
vapour trail,
becomes a unicorn.

I see faces, if I squint a little,
and if faces had three eyes
and two noses.

I see shapeless blobs
that could be monsters
from old sci-fi shows.

I see all these things and more
as I stare out of this hospice window,
waiting... just waiting...
until I join those clouds too.

Heart Beat

By Farha A. Ja eel

It was a winter afternoon in December, 2015. The roads were covered in a layer of powdery snow, undisturbed, from the previous night's snowfall. I strolled down the path in the neighbourhood and looked around. Houses with snow-capped rooftops and shovelled paths leading to the doorstep. Wreaths hung on the doors. Cars were parked in their respective driveways. Inside, elders were seated by the warm, glowing fire, steaming mugs of hot cocoa in hand. Little children, played with their pets, or amongst themselves. Potted fern trees stood in a corner, decorated with stars and guardian angels. The playground in the neighbourhood was completely deserted, swing sets and merry-go-round creaking as they moved with the cool afternoon breeze. Everyone was home for the holidays.

I let out a breath, I didn't realise I had been holding. It had been a year since that fateful day. I could still remember my mother crying as I was rushed to the hospital, the beeping of the equipment in the operation theatre, just as I lost consciousness.

Having been born with a weak heart, my parents had been cautioned against making me feel tired or excited. As a child, I always felt left out. At school, I was excluded from outdoor activities or sports, as a result of my condition. My health deteriorated as I got older, and things got considerably worse last year. The doctors said that I needed to undergo a heart transplant as soon as possible.

I never got to meet my donor. I only knew him by his name - Matt. His family had unanimously agreed to the surgery, for which I'll be forever grateful.

I adjusted the collar of my jacket, as a gust of wind blew, dishevelling my hair. Tucking my hands in my jeans pocket, I made my way to the graveyard. It had been a year since he had died, and I was given a second chance to live.

Opening the gate, I made my way into the churchyard and saw rows of tombstones. I hadn't been here to visit him before. I made my way through the tombstones, reading them as I went. That's when I heard it - a sob. At first I thought I was imagining things, but I was curious to find the source of the sound. I turned around, and saw two rows ahead of me, a girl kneeling in front of a gravestone, her hands cradling her face and shoulders shaking with unrelenting sobs. She was dressed in black and her shoulder-length auburn hair was pulled into a low ponytail.

My heart lurched when I saw her. It was strange. I had never felt anything like it before. I felt a need to comfort her, although I didn't know who she was.

I walked towards her. Having been alerted of my presence by the sound of crunching snow beneath my shoes; she looked up. My heart skipped a beat. She had the most beautiful pair of ocean blue eyes, I'd ever seen, brimming with emotion. Then I took in the rest of her appearance. Her skin was pale, her cheeks rosy, tear tracks ran down her face and her eyes were red-rimmed.

She apologized, because she hadn't realised that she was not alone. I smiled, and let her know that it was alright; that I was just passing by. Then I looked down at the gravestone, which read:

"Matthew Lucas Smith
September 12th, 1987 - December 23rd, 2014"

She must have noticed the look of surprise on my face, because she looked at me questioningly. I told her that I had come to visit him. Then it was her turn to look surprised. I sat down beside her, and we talked about how we had both known him.

Matt was Sarah's fiancé. She met him in college and they fell in love. They were engaged in October 2014, and were to be wedded in Spring 2015. He had gone away on a business trip and was planning to return before Christmas. He was on his way home when he met with an accident. He was rushed to the hospital. Due to the heavy injuries to his head, he was declared brain-dead.

When his family was told about the urgent need of a donor, they had agreed to it; because it was what he would have wanted.

We sat in silence for a few minutes. She showed me a photo of him, taken a few months before his untimely death. We bade farewell and parted ways.

That night, I didn't fall asleep. My mind was pre-occupied with my encounter with Sarah. From the moment I saw her, I sensed a feeling of familiarity. It was strange, because that was the first time I had ever met her.

A few weeks later, we ran into each other again. This time, at a bookstore a few blocks away from home. We had a lengthy conversation at a coffee house next door. We got to know a lot about each other; our likes and dislikes, our interests; things we had in common.

We started meeting each other regularly. The more time we spent together, the more we were drawn closer to each other. A few months later, we were officially dating.

Every time I think back to the first time I met her, I remember how my heart skipped a beat when I saw her, and how the sound of her voice always made my heart race.

Every encounter afterwards, had me feeling the same way. I never thought that I would meet her again. But, somehow, I just felt that I had to be at the bookstore that day. Being at the coffee house too, stirred a strong feeling of familiarity. Later, I learnt that, that was where Sarah and Matt used to often meet.

I then realised that, me showing up at the graveyard a year after Matt died, and again at the bookshop, was no mere coincidence. We were meant to meet, so that Sarah could let go of Matt and move on, and the both of us could find closure.

The familiarity, the rapid heart beat every time I was with her, is because the heart *always* remembers.

A Cry For Spring

By Barbara E. Robinson

The trees that summer kissed are bare and still,
hold empty arms out to the wintry sky
for autumn stole the leaves, turned them to mould,
strewn around each bole and left to die.
A solemn sight to drown my heart in sorrow,
to wrap my soul in shadows of darkest greys
for winter days are now so sad and careworn,
I cannot find a song to sing in praise.

If I could feel once more the summer sun
beyond the cold north wind, the snow and ice,
then I would maybe lose this melancholia
and find my own sweet piece of paradise.
Both swift and swallow flew so long ago,
left crows to caw their song of pending doom,
a harsh sound in the quiet of the dawn,
Oh skylark please come sing your welcome tune.

First published in Dial 174 magazine.

Contributors...

ABIGAIL GEORGE

Abigail is a blogger on Goodreads, a short story writer, a feminist, and a full-time poet. She is hard at work on a young adult novel. She briefly studied speech and drama and film. She was the recipient of writing grants from the National Arts Council in Johannesburg, Centre for the Book in Cape Town, and the Eastern Cape Provincial Arts and Culture Council in East London, South Africa. Her literary work (fiction) was nominated for the Pushcart Prize. She lives in the Eastern Cape, South Africa. She has been published widely in print and online in South Africa, as well as abroad and has written for *Modern Diplomacy* and contributed to a symposium on *Ovi Magazine: Finland's English Online Magazine*. Abigail has contributed to *TRAVEL, LONELY, WAR, HAPPY* and *BETRAYAL*.
E: abigailgeorge79@gmail.com

AKANKSHA BHATNAGAR

Akanksha Bhatnagar holds ties with a very important place in India's history, known as Gwalior (MP) today. She is pursuing a BSc in computer science from Kamla Raja girls college, Madhya Pradesh, India. She has a very supportive family background and since childhood Akanksha has always wanted to do something in the writing field, and has lots of words and feelings which she expresses by writing; this very promising and studious writer has won many competitions in different fields, and has been published in many national and international anthologies.
E: akankshab0111@gmail.com
Instagram: tang ble_abstraction

BARBARA E ROBINSON

"I live in the picturesque English town of Whitby – of Dracula renown. I have had an interest in writing since my early school days when I won a prize for a short story which was published it *The Daily Mirror*. After winning the Wetherby prize at the Literary Festival in 1985, I was later short-listed for the Leeds Peace poetry competition and then won the Partners Open Poetry Competition. My writing, published in many small press magazines and anthologies, covers a broad range of both adult and children's poetry and prose and I've recorded stories for Wetherby local radio. My work is also being published in *Australia's Free Xpression* and India's *Metverse Muse*. I have had three poetry books published; *One Moment in Time, Singing to the Four Winds* and *A Touch of Nature* (2013). Also, I contributed to the World War 1 anthology *Whitby Voices* for Whitby's

Pannett Park Art Gallery. My current project, together with five members of the Library writing group, is a book entitled: *A Journey Through The Museum*, a tour in poetry and prose through the James Cook Museum at Whitby - now gone to print. I have recently finished a humorous children's poetry book which hopefully will be published soon." Barbara has also contributed to *WAR, HAPPY* and *BETRAYAL*.
E: moonberry1@live.co.uk

BEATON GALAFA

Beaton is a Malawian writer of poetry, fiction and non-fiction. He holds a Bachelor's Degree in Education (Language) from the University of Malawi, Chancellor College. His works have appeared in international literary journals such as *The Maynard, South 85 Journal, Birds Piled Loosely, The Voices Project* and *Bhashabandhan Literary Review*. He was one of the twelve East African emerging writers who attended the Commonwealth Creative Non-fiction Writers' Workshop in Kampala, Uganda. In 2016, his essay *Strategies for Achieving Trans-Generational Leadership in Political Parties* in Malawi won the 2016 Free Expression Institute-Malawi Essay Writing Competition. He was selected to be one of the mentees in the 2017 Writivism Literary Project for the Koffi Addo Nonfiction Writing Contest for African emerging writers. His essay got an honorable mention in the 2017 SEALOEarth Global Essay Contest. He is the current chairperson for Pen Avenue Malawi and the Founding Editor of a Malawian online literary magazine. Beaton has also contributed to *BETRAYAL*.

BERNADETTE PEREZ

A poet possessing expression and creativity. In 1990 Bernadette received the Silver Poet Award from World of Poetry. Her work has appeared in *The Wishing Well; Musings* in 2010, *Small Canyons* anthology in 2013, *Poems 4 Peace* in 2014. *Fix and Free* anthology in 2015. She is the Vice President of the New Mexico State Poetry Society and member of Rio Grande Valencia Poets since 2005. Bernadette has contributed to *TRAVEL, LOVE, WAR, HAPPY* and *BETRAYAL*.
E: bpburritos@aol.com

BILL COX

Bill is from Aberdeen, Scotland, where he resides with his partner and her daughter. He started writing in 2014 after he had to give up his first love, hillwalking, because his knees couldn't take it anymore. Though he misses the mountain tops, he has found some solace in the written word and its ability to take him to all sorts of interesting places. Bill has also contributed to *BETRAYAL*.
E: malphesius@yahoo.com

BRIAN LANGLEY

"I live in suburban Perth, the capital of Western Australia with my wife of fifty plus years. I write Bush Poetry, Australian rhyming poetry which has near perfect metre and consistency of structure. I write across many subjects and perform (mostly from memory) regularly at retirement villages, aged care facilities, country festivals, service and social clubs etc., etc. I perform under the name The City Poet - this is due to me being a member of the Western Australian Bush Poets Association, many members of which have a rural background and write on rural subjects - most of my poetry is from the point of view of an Australian city dweller. My poems reflect my lifestyle, age and interests, mainly ageing, being Australian, the environment, travelling, fishing and contemporary living. I also delve occasionally into politics and history. I have self published several books as well as some audio CDs and a couple of e-books of historic Western Australian poetry. I was born in rural Western Australia but came to the city in my teens. Following a career in telecommunications, I retired and started writing a family history. I found that I had a poet (Leigh Hunt) in my ancestry and looked up his work. I was far from impressed and thought I could do better, so I commenced writing, mostly contemplative short poems. - that was back in the mid 1990s. Since then my poetry has changed direction somewhat, now being mostly classified as Australian Bush Poetry." Brian has contributed to *TRAVEL, WAR* and *LOVE*.

E: briandot@tpg.com.au

W: Brianlangley.wabushpoets.asn.au

BRIGETTE FURLONGER

Writer and photographer Brigette, has enjoyed creating for as long as she can remember. Her love of writing has blossomed over the past ten years. As a mother, wife, sister, traveller and a nature lover, Brigette has new material to explore at her fingertips. Also, she feels her writing and photography are symbiotic, and encourage new creations everyday. It has only been recently that she has become more public with her work. Over the last few years, Brigette's photography and writing have been in several shows and books. Her accomplishments include winning the People's Choice Award for a short story submitted to the *Duncan Journal,* being short-listed for a nationwide poetry competition, and being one of the contributors and photographers for Word and Vision. Brigette has contributed to *LOVE* and *WAR*.

E: bcfurlonger@gmail.com

Blog: Saanichinletphotosblog.wordpress.com

CHRYS SALT

Chrys is a trained performer and broadcaster, as well as widely published and anthologized poet. She has read and performed at festivals across the UK in Europe, North America, Finland and India, and won numerous awards including a National Media Award (CRS), a New Writing Bursary (English Arts Council), a Work Development Grant (Scottish Arts Council), and a Fringe First from The Edinburgh Festival. She has published seven books for actors (Pub: Methuen Drama) and eight poetry collections. In 2012 *The Burning* was selected as one of the 20 Best Scottish Poems. In 2014 her pamphlet *Weaver of Grass* was shortlisted for the Callum MacDonald Memorial Award, she received Creative Scotland Bursary to finish her last collection *Dancing on a Rock* (Pub: IDP), and was awarded an MBE in the Queen's Birthday Honours List for Services to The Arts. She is listed in Who's Who. Chrys has also contributed to *BETRAYAL* and *WAR*.

E: Chrys@chryssalt.com
W: Chryssalt.com

CLARE LIGHTFOOT

"I live and work as a therapist and artist on the beautiful island of Malta. Prior to this I lived in Saudi Arabia and Bahrain for many years. I am an artist and a poet working through blessings and prayers and, before I write or paint, I pray and ask for the angels to be with me." Clare has also contributed to *LOVE* and *BETRAYAL.*

E: clarelightfoot2012@gmail.com

CLARE ROSLINGTON

Clare has always loved writing since childhood, as her main creative expression. She writes from her heart, inspired by nature and her love for her devoted fiancé. She fell in love with him initially by reading his beautiful poetry, then they met a week later when he came from Sweden to where she lives in England. They are currently writing a book of love poetry together at their home by the Malvern Hills. Clare has a daily meditation and yoga practice, and does gardening for others. She also enjoys the creative flow of painting heart art and seascapes with watercolours and acrylics. She has a gift for nature photography which often complements her writing and poetry. She has written a wealth of poetry, prose and children's short stories which she shares with others to inspire a deep connection with nature and to help find inner peace. Clare has also contributed to *TRAVEL* and *HAPPY*.

E.: claredelphine@gmail.com
FB: Clare Roslington

COURTNEY SPEEDY

Courtney is a poet from Whangarei, New Zealand. She has had her poetry published in two separate collections; *Re-Draft: The Word Is Out* (2014) and *Write Off Line: They Came in From the Dark* (2014) Her inspiration comes from the world around her, and music in particular. She is working towards self-publishing a collection of her poetry and prose in the near future. Courtney has also contributed to *LONELY, LOVE, WAR, HAPPY* and *BETRAYAL.*

E: courtneyleoniejayne@gmail.com

DAVID HOLLYWOOD

David lives in Ireland and is married with four children. His particular interest is in developing a public enthusiasm for poetry among those who aspire too appreciate the genre, but haven't yet made the leap into writing or proclaiming their verse. As a result, he founded and for four years directed'The Colours of Life poetry festival's in Bahrain, and subsequently worked upon the same in Antigua, The West Indies, before bringing it to Waterford upon his return to Ireland. He is the author of an eclectic collection of poems titled *Waiting Spaces* plus contributed to *My Beautiful Bahrain, Poetic Bahrain, More of My Beautiful Bahrain* and was the in-house poet for *Bahrain Confidential* magazine and, as a result, he is one of the most widely read Western poets in The Middle East. He is also a regular literary critic for *Taj Mahal Review,* plus an essayist on the subject of poetry appreciation. He has been accredited with membership of The Society of Classical Poets. There are plans for a new collection of poetry and essays to be released shortly. David has an additional responsibility for the teaching of Wine Appreciation Programmes and Themes which he has developed for the hospitality industry. David has also contributed to *TRAVEL, LONELY, LOVE, WAR, HAPPY* and *BETRAYAL.*

E: davidhollywood23@hotmail.com
W: www.thewineappreciationsociety.ie

DAVID WATT

David is a Canberra, Australia based writer who enjoys creating thought-provoking poems. His poetry can be found on The Society of Classical Poets website and in *THE EMPATH – The Magazine for Highly Sensitive People*. His children's poem entitled *The Clutterbucks* received a highly commended award as judged by a panel of primary school children for the 2015 CJ Denis Poetry Competition in Toolangi, Victoria. David received a certificate of commendation for his poem *Shades of Mollymook* in the 2016 Henry Lawson Society Literary Awards. His poetic response entitled *The Square on Tlomackie* appeared on Wall of Life as part of a nation-wide project for 27 January 2017 Holocaust Memorial Day Trust commemorations.

David has contributed to *TRAVEL, LOVE, WAR, HAPPY* and *BETRAYAL*.
E: maridav@wattfor.net

DON ADAMS
Don was in the education field for forty years until an accident prompted his retirement, when he then turned to writing. He has participated in various poetry and short story competitions with some success, and featured a few times in the Award Winning Australian Writers annual publication. Don has also contributed to *BETRAYAL, WAR, TRAVEL* and *LOVE*.
E: theldon@paradise.net.nz

FARHA A. JALEEL
"I was born and brought up in Bahrain. I currently live in Sri Lanka. I started out writing short stories at the age of eight and have been passionate about it ever since. I started writing poems a few years ago. I have had one of my short stories published in a local newspaper in Sri Lanka, and hope to get more of my work published in the future." Farha has also contributed to *LONELY, LOVE* and *BETRAYAL*.
E: crimson_rose97@yahoo.com

GABRIELLA GAROFALO
Born in Italy some decades ago, Gabriella fell in love with the English language at six when she started writing poems (in Italian), and is the author of *Lo sguardo di Orfeo, L'inverno di vetro, Di altre stelle polari* and *Blue branches*.
E: grrz2001@yahoo.it

GREG BOGAERTS
Greg is a writer who lives in Buttaba, Australia. He has had five books of fiction and more than three hundred and fifty stories published. He is married to Jill and once had a cat called Whisper. Greg has also contributed to *TRAVEL, LOVE, WAR* and *BETRAYAL*.
E: gregbogaerts54@gmail.com

JASMINE KANG
Jasmine is an American writer currently based in California. Although she mostly writes inspirational prose and poetry, she also expresses herself through art and photography. Her work has been published and recognized internationally. Besides art and writing, she also enjoys nature and listening to music.
E: jasminekk@gmail.com
W: Moonshinegarden.com

JENNIFER RIGGS

Jennifer was born in Tanzania, childhood in wartime England, girlhood in Zanzibar, married life in Kenya (in the thick of Mau Mau terrorism), and now in Australia. Her writing experiences include: editorial (scientific); contributions to national and international conferences and journals (educational); reviewing (Fiction Focus); broadcasts (ABC Radio National) a novel *The Late Mr. Collins* and an anthology for the bereaved *A Handful of Lilies*. Also devising and hosting writers' workshops and the perennial pleasure of just writing, including poetry – but who wants poetry? Thank goodness you do! Jennifer has also contributed to *LOVE, TRAVEL, WAR, HAPPY* and *BETRAYAL*.
E: riggsclues@bigpond.com

JOHN KARL STOKES

John is internationally known as one of Australia's most courageous and innovative of authors, poets, essayists and librettists writing in English. He has won and been short or long-listed for many prizes, including the UC Vice-Chancellor's International, and Montreal International. He has been published in many journals; tutored in literature; and read his work worldwide. His books include: *A River in the Dark* (2003) and the prize-winning *Fire in the Afternoon*, (Halstead, 2015). John has also contributed to *LOVE, TRAVEL, WAR HAPPY* and *BETRAYAL*.
E: johnstokespoet@me.com
W: Johnkarlstokes.com

JOHN R. SABINE

John is into his third career: first a scientist and academic, then a business consultant / entrepreneur and now a 'Scholar-at-Large' (thinker, writer, speaker, actor). His recent publications include a major travel memoir, *Around the World in Eighty Ways*, a collection of short stores, *Look Alive: the long and the short of it*, and two of poetry, as well as several individual poems, short stories and essays. His acting activities include stage, film and television work – and especially in his stage persona, *Old Jack: the Aussie Gleeman* (purveyor of tall tales, short stories and pithy poetry). John has also contributed to *TRAVEL, LOVE* and *BETRAYAL*.
E: jsabine@iimetro.com.au
W: www.jsabine.com

JOHN TUNALEY

"I was born in Manchester, England to parents who met while doing war work. Dad was a smelter on a furnace, Mam operated an overhead crane that carried the containers of molten steel, but only after she moved from her job in city centre where she helped sew

barrage balloons. 'Too much bombing there' was her considered opinion. Two Australian uncles fought in New Guinea, my mother's youngest brother was a sailor in the Suez Canal crisis. All this informs my writing (over fifty years and counting)." John has also contributed to *WAR, HAPPY* and *BETRAYAL.*
E: johntunaley@yahoo.co.uk

JUSTIN FOX
Justin is a writer and photographer based in Cape Town, South Africa. He's a former editor of *Getaway International* travel magazine. Justin was a Rhodes Scholar and received a doctorate in English from Oxford University after which he became a research fellow at the University of Cape Town, where he now teaches part-time. His articles and photographs have appeared internationally in a number of publications and on a wide range of topics, while his short stories and poems have appeared in various anthologies. His recent books include *The Marginal Safari* (Umuzi, 2010), *Whoever Fears the Sea* (Umuzi, 2014) and *The Impossible Five* (Tafelberg, 2015). Justin has contributed to *TRAVEL, LOVE* and *WAR.*
E: justinfoxafrica@gmail.com

KAPARDELI EFTICHIA
Dr. Eftichia has a Doctorate from Arts and Culture World Academy. Born in Athens and lives in Patras, she writes poetry, stories, short stories, xai-kou, essays and novels. She studied journalism AKEM (Athenian training centre), University of Cyprus in Greek culture. She has many awards in national competitions and is a member of the IWA (International Writers) and The World Poets Society. Dr. Eftichia has also contributed to *WAR, HAPPY* and *BETRAYAL.*
E: kapardeli@gmail.com
FB: Facebook.com/kapardeli.eftichia

KATHLEEN BLEAKLEY
Descended from lighthouse keepers, Kathleen lives in Wollongong, Australia, between the sea and the escarpment. Kathleen's poem/s are from *Lightseekers*, her third book and second major collaboration with 'pling. Their previous publication is *Jumping Out Of Cars* with Andrea Gawthorne. Kathleen was born in Morocco on a Thursday. "Thursday's child has far to go..." Kathleen has also contributed to *LOVE, TRAVEL* and *WAR.*
E: kathleen@pling.id.au
W: Ginninderrapress.org.au/poetry
FB: Lightseekers via 'pling Px

KATHLEEN BOYLE

Kathleen Boyle nee Dodd, was born in Liverpool, where she spent her childhood years before leaving to train as a teacher in Hull in 1972. Kathleen has worked as a teacher in Hull, Leeds, London and Carlisle, and international schools in Columbia, Bahrain, Cairo and Vietnam. She has written stories and poems throughout her life and published a collection of poems about growing up in 1950s Liverpool entitled, *Sugar Butties and Mersey Memoirs*, as well as a collection of poems for children about a teddy bear called *Harry Pennington* in 2008. During her time in Bahrain she wrote *The Pearl House*, a short story which spans the cultural divides of Liverpool and Bahrain. The story, together with her poems, *Bahrain* and *Umm Al Hassam* were published in *My Beautiful Bahrain* and *More of My Beautiful Bahrain*. Kathleen has written a series of children's stories for Beirut publishers Dar El Fikr, two of which, *The Jewel of the Deep* and *The Magic Pearl and Dilmun*, have now been illustrated and published. She has written a novella, *Catherine of Liverpool*, completed and published while she was teaching in Cairo, together with her poems *Alexandria* and *Bolivia*. She is presently working on a sequel to *Catherine of Liverpool*. A mother of three and grandmother of two, she is now into her fifth decade as a teacher, combining her love of writing, painting and travel with teaching and is currently working in Vietnam. Kath has also contributed to *LONELY, LOVE, TRAVEL HAPPY* and *BETRAYAL*.
E: kathdodd@aol.com

KIRSTY A. NIVEN

Kirsty lives in Dundee, Scotland with her husband and cat. She graduated from the University of Dundee with a first class English degree. She was a featured poet on *Creekwalker* and her work has appeared in *Artificial Womb* and on *Mothers Always Write*. One of her poems is also currently on the Scottish Book Trust's website as part of their Secrets & Confessions project. Her poetry is due to appear in *The Dawntreader, Sarasvati* and the anthology *I Only Wanted One Time To See You Laughing*, as well as appearing for a second time on *Mothers Always Write* in the near future. Kirsty has also contributed to *LOVE, WAR, HAPPY* and BETRAYAL.
E: kaniven13@outlook.com

LINDA-ANN LO SCHIAVO

Native New Yorker, LindaAnn is currently completing her second documentary film on Texas Guinan (1884-1933) and the Prohibition Era in America. Her work has been seen onstage, onscreen, and in many publications such as *Metamorphose Magazine, Measure, Italian-Americana, Atavic, The Bacon Review*, and *Nous*. LindaAnn has also

contributed to *HAPPY, WAR* and *BETRAYAL.*
E: nonstopny@aol.com
T: @Mae_Westside
Blog: TexasGuinan.blogspot.com

LINDA M. CRATE

Linda is a Pennsylvanian native born in Pittsburgh yet raised in the rural town of Conneautville. Her poetry, short stories, articles, and reviews have been published in a myriad of magazines both online and in print. She has three published chapbooks *A Mermaid Crashing Into Dawn* (Fowlpox Press - June 2013), *Less Than A Man* (The Camel Saloon - January 2014), and *If Tomorrow Never Comes* (Scars Publications, August 2016). Her fantasy novel *Blood & Magic* was published in March 2015. The second novel of this series *Dragons & Magic* was published in October 2015. The third of the seven book series *Centaurs & Magic* was published November 2016. Her novels *Corvids & Magic* and *Phoenix Tears* are forthcoming. Linda has also contributed to *WAR, HAPPY* and *BETRAYAL.*
E: veritaserumvial@hotmail.com
FB: Facebook.com/Linda-M-Crate-129813357119547
Blog: Bloodandmagic.blogspot.com

LYNETTE CUPIDO

"I have been writing poems since schooling for family and friends on special occasions. I would like to take my writing to the next level of short stories or novels. I love writing poems as it gives me the rush of letting go of emotions that I sometime hide or don't express much. Writing gives me the freedom to be someone else for that moment when I want to hide from this world." Lynette has also contributed to *HAPPY* and *BETRAYAL.*
E: lynette.cupido41@gmail.com

MADHAVI TIWARY

"My first rendezvous with writing was at college. My scribbling, which I fondly called 'poems', was proudly and regularly passed on to the like-minded class mates. We would exchange the little slips, dubbing them 'data' in the psychology class and savour each other's badly cooked write ups. After about four years of such expressions of passionate thoughts, there came a grand lull in my writing. Laundry lists, love and hate letters replaced all that writers' pride – 'data'. It took a decade for me to pick up writing again with zeal and zest. As a result, in the past few years I have written about fifty articles which were published in the editorial columns. I have written as many poems many of which are still hatching in the warmth of my private closet. My articles were invariably written when I hungered to share

my thoughts with the world. However, most of my poems were the direct consequence of some kind of personal flood happening in my heart. My most cherished aspiration is publishing a joint book of my daughter's, and my, write-ups. A subsidiary dream, life permitting, is to write a book which could summarize my life's emotions in the form of a story that will leave the readers with a smile in their heart and with a storm in their minds." Madhavi has contributed to *LONELY*, *TRAVEL* and *HAPPY*.
E: madhavi.dwivedi@gmail.com

MANTZ YORKE
Mantz lives in Manchester, England. His poems have appeared in a number of print magazines, anthologies and e-magazines in the UK, Ireland, Israel, Canada, the US and Hong Kong. Mantz has also contributed to *WAR* and *BETRAYAL*.
E: mantzyorke@mantzyorke.plus.com

MARY ANNE ZAMMIT
Mary Anne is a graduate from the University of Malta in Social Work, in Probation Services, in Diplomatic Studies and in Masters in Probation. Mary Anne has also obtained a Diploma in Freelance and Feature Writing from the London School of Journalism. Mary Anne paints, writes poetry, novels and articles both in Maltese and in English and is the author of three fiction books in Maltese; the first book was *Id-Dell ta' l-Eżmeraldi*, and *Ir-Raġel l-Iswed*, the latter was awarded a prize by MAPA (Maltese Association of Authors and Publishers) This was followed by a fiction book with the title *Stupru (Rape)*. In 2005 Marie Anne attended for a script writing workshop in Sitges, Spain. The book was presented in the literary section in the festival; Woman Creators of the Two Seas. Woman and Tradition, held in Thessaloniki, Greece between the 28 August and 04 September 2006. The Festival was organized by the Unesco Centre for Women and Peace in the Balkans. In 2008 the novel *Torn Velvet* was published and exhibited at the New Title Show Case at the London Book Fair between the 14 and 16 April 2008. The same book was published by the Mental Health Group with the title *Shattered Wings*. In 2009 Mary Anne's fourth book in Maltese *Tfal Misruqa, (Kidnapped Children)* a novel about the reality of missing children and child pornography, was published. In 2009 the Marie Anne's short story *My Son, My Past* was highly commended in the Aesthetica Annual Creative Competition UK. In 2010 two poems were published in the Strand book for International Poetry by Strand Publishers UK. In 2015, the novel *Dawn in Seville* was published. In 2015 one of Mary Anne's poem has been set to music and performed during the Mdina Cathedral Art Biennale by Maestro Reuben Pace. Mary Anne's

literary work was also featured in Literature Today, Volumes 4,5 and 6. Other two poems were published in 2016 in *Taj Mahal Review Volume 15,* published by Cyberwit India. One other poem was published in the *New English Verse* in 2016, and in *Praxis* online magazine for Arts and Literature. Mary Anne has also contributed to *WAR* and *BETRAYAL.*
E: mariefrances3@gmail.com

MARY COONS
Mary works with professionals who want to communicate more clearly in the marketplace. She does this through writing. Mary also works with different entities who want to leave a lasting legacy by documenting their family stories and histories. Mary is the award-winning author of *Culturally Speaking: Promoting Cross-Cultural Awareness in a Post-9/11 World* - a finalist for two U.S. book awards for literary excellence. Mary has also contributed to *WAR.*
E: marycoons@usinternet.com
W: Marycoons.com

MAVIS ATHA
Mavis has also contributed to *TRAVEL.*
E: mavisatha@gmail.com

OLIVIA MATTHEWS
Olivia is a twelve year-old, currently attending Morrinsville Intermediate in the Waikato, NZ. She loves writing war prose which is fuelled from her passion of reading anything war related. She is in the proud possession of her great Grandfather's war medals from WW2 and loves to attend the ANZAC day ceremonies. Olivia has had her work published in the *Toitoi Anzac Special Issue Writing Journal.* Olivia has also contributed to *WAR.*
E: wayneandalison@xtra.co.nz

PAMELA SCOTT
Pamela lives in Glasgow, UK with her partner. Her poems and stories have been published in various magazines including *The New Writer, Carillon* and *Words with Jam.* Her poems have been published in anthologies by Indigo Dreams Press including *Crab Lines off the Pier.* Her poems and stories have won 2nd and 3rd place in various competitions including the Newark Poetry Society Competition and the Global Short Story Competition. She has completed two novels and is seeking publication / representation, and is working on a third novel and a series of short stories inspired by the seven deadly sins. Pamela has also contributed to *TRAVEL, LOVE, WAR, HAPPY* and *BETRAYAL.*

E: pamelascottwriter@yahoo.com
W: Pamelascottwriter.com
W: Pscottwritingnotebook.wordpress.com
FB: Facebook.com/pamelascottwriter
T: Twitter.com/pscottwriter
Blog: Thebookloversboudoir.wordpress.com

REBECCA SUTTON

"I am from Auckland, New Zealand. I have a degree in philosophy and politics, and am currently doing a Masters in Theology. I have been interested in writing poetry ever since my teens, but have only recently starting to write poetry again. I am involved in a poetry group in the town where I live, and my aim is to continue to write more poetry in 2017." Rebecca has also contributed to *WAR* and *BETRAYAL*.
E: rsut80@yahoo.co.nz

ROSEMARY RIGSBY

"I was born in Duncan, British Columbia, Canada, and lived my childhood and teen years in logging camps and small towns on Vancouver Island. After high school in Lake Cowichan, I attended the University of Victoria, and a few years later moved to the City of Vancouver. I worked, raised my family, and upon 'retirement,' I re-enrolled full-time in university to further my interest in writing. In 2014, I published *Prairie Seas, Mountain Harvest*, a biography/memoir. I am presently a resident of Delta, B.C where I work on other writing projects, when not being wife, mother, and 'Granny'." Rosemary has also contributed to *WAR*.
E: rrigsby@telus.net

SARA MADAN

"I write what my heart feels or my eyes have seen (non-fiction and fiction) to empower myself and along the way inspire others to do something differently. I am a member of Bahrain Writers Circle, as well as member of many NGO's in Bahrain. I wear many hats, and one of them is volunteering in various capacities (i.e. writing press releases, editing magazines, managing events, projects and website content management, serving on executive committees etc..,) By profession I am a Certified Public Accountant." Sara has also contributed to *BETRAYAL*.
E: o.madan@gmail.com

S'BUSISO MANQA

S'busiso is a South African born Poet, author and film-maker, who has recently published a book titled: *Understanding Life Through*

Poetry (2016), and is currently a creative director in a media company based in South Africa called Octopus Vision. He has also collaborated in humanitarian projects with the International Association of Scientologists to inspire change in the townships of South Africa. S'busiso has also contributed to *LOVE, TRAVEL, WAR, HAPPY* and *BETRAYAL.*

E: sbusisomanqa@gmail.com

SOURABH ACHARYA

A person of words, aspirations, and full of dreams. Perseverant, dedicated, and passionate enough for whatever he wishes to achieve. Hailing from a small town, dreams seem a real big deal for a guy as such. In love with words since three years now, and the feeling seems manifolding itself with each passing moment. Calls himself a Wordlust, and the one who can sacrifice a life for words. Writes in multiple languages, English, Hindi, and Urdu being some of them. A nineteen year old, finding his way out through the worldly menaces.

E: sourabh310398@gmail.com

STELLA CARRUTHERS

"From Aotearoa New Zealand I am a writer and information studies student with a passion for sustainable living. My writing style is lyrical and always poetic and expresses a deep love of imagery and metaphor. As a writer, you could say I like to paint pictures with words. The density of description in my work reflects this ideology. I am an avid journal keeper, a keen knitter and vegetarian cook who loves to drink a lot of tea and who takes pride in being owned by two elderly cats." Stella has also contributed to *BETRAYAL.*

E: stellacarr20@gmail.com

T: twitter.com/Stellabelle20

LinkedIn: Linkedin.com/in/stella-carruthers-3b0bb7118/

TERRY HICKLAND

"I am a Northern Ireland based writer of crime, general fiction and poetry, and am married with one son. During the 1980s, I moved to Germany, where I lived in Braunschweig, Lower Saxony, for a time, before finally settling in Wolfsburg. As a result, I am fluent in German. Upon my return home, I created a number of successful commercial ventures before accepting a lecturing post at a local college. I have been studying at the University of Ulster for the past two years, as part of my postgraduate degree in teaching - which I completed in June of this year - receiving a commendation for my work. When I'm not writing, I like attending literary and classical music events, and working on German classic cars."

E: terryjohn60@outlook.com

W: Terryhickland.co.uk

TRACY DAVIDSON
Tracy lives in Warwickshire, England, and writes poetry and flash fiction. Her work has appeared in various publications and anthologies, including: *Poet's Market* (2015), *Mslexia, Writing Magazine, The Binnacle, Modern Haiku, A Hundred Gourds, Atlas Poetica, Journey to Crone, Ekphrastia Gone Wild, The Great Gatsby Anthology, The Garden,* and *In Protest: 150 Poems for Human Rights.* Tracy has also contributed to *WAR.*
E: james0309@btinternet.com

BETRAYAL - A Collection of Poetry and Prose on Betrayal and Being Betrayed

The SIXTH in the Collections of Poetry and Prose book series.

BETRAYAL not only covers emotional betrayal and infidelity, but betrayal at work, in health, at war, with life and the betrayal of addiction.

With many of the contributions reflecting the diverse backgrounds and cultures of the writers, in BETRAYAL there are 128 contributions from 60 writers in 24 countries; Antigua, Australia, Bahrain, Bhutan, Canada, England, Greece, India, Japan, Kenya, Malawi, Malaysia, Malta, Mexico, New Zealand, Nigeria, Poland, Republic of Ireland, Scotland, South Africa, Sri Lanka, Tanzania, USA and Vietnam, all exploring the themes of betrayal and being betrayed.

BETRAYAL is a unique collection of poetry and short prose from some of the most talented and inspirational writers around the world.

Paperback £9.99 (GBP). ISBN: 978-1545417737
Kindle £3.99 (GBP). ASIN: B071WG36FW

HAPPY - A Collection of Poetry and Prose on Happiness and Being Happy

The FIFTH in the Collections of Poetry and Prose book series.

What makes people happy? What is happiness? Can happiness be found from people, places and things around us, or is it purely internal – a reflection and result of our own thoughts, feelings, attitude and mindset? Can we really be as happy as we want to be?

With many of the contributions reflecting the diverse backgrounds and cultures of the writers, in HAPPY there are 129 contributions from 60 writers in 21 countries: Antigua, Australia, Bahrain, Canada, England, France, Greece, Indonesia, Ireland, Kenya, Malaysia, Mexico, New Zealand, Nigeria, Puerto Rica, Scotland, South Africa, Sri Lanka, Uganda, USA and Vietnam, all exploring themes of happiness and being happy.

HAPPY is a unique collection of poetry and short prose from some of the most talented and inspirational writers around the world.

Paperback £9.99 (GBP). ISBN: 978-1542482264
Kindle £3.99 (GBP). ASIN: B06XDQPG38

WAR - A Collection of Poetry and Prose on the Bravery and Horror of War

The FOURTH in the Collections of Poetry and Prose book series.

With many of the contributions reflecting the diverse backgrounds and cultures of the writers, in WAR there are 170 contributions from 77 writers in 29 countries as diverse as Bahrain and Bolivia, England and India.

Covering the two World Wars, the wars in the Middle East, Africa and Asia, conflicts in the Balkans, Eastern Europe and Ireland, as well as historical wars, war in general, PTSD, the side-effects of war and much, much more... WAR - A Collection of Poetry and Prose on the Bravery and Horror of War is a thought-provoking, moving and often harrowing, yet also occasionally heart-warming and uplifting collection of poetry and short prose from some of the most talented and inspirational writers around the world.

Paperback £9.99 (GBP). ISBN: 978-1539565888
Kindle £3.99 (GBP). ASIN: B01N6NETRR

TRAVEL - A Collection of Poetry and Prose on Travels and Travelling

The THIRD in the Collections of Poetry and Prose book series.

From a bleak bus ride through Glasgow at midnight, to a trans - Californian road trip, from summer in Dubrovnik and finding peace in a Spanish paradise, to a bumpy bus ride to Kampala and the Paris Metro at night... TRAVEL, the third of the Collections of Poetry and Prose book series, features 97 contributions from 46 writers and poets around the world, all writing in their own unique, wonderful and occasionally quirky way about their travels and experiences travelling.

TRAVEL explores the world and its people and culture in an undeniably unique and fascinating way.

Paperback £9.99 (GBP). ISBN: 978-1535080767
Kindle £3.99 (GBP). ASIN: B01M2WZJIA

LOVE - A Collection of Poetry and Prose on Loving and Being in Love

The SECOND in the Collections of Poetry and Prose book series.

LOVE - A Collection of Poetry and Prose on Loving and Being in Love features 194 contributions from 86 writers and poets around the world, all writing in their own unique, wonderful and occasionally quirky way about loving and being in love.

From rural towns and villages in Africa, Asia and India, and the tiny islands of Bahrain and Shetland, to the bustling metropolises of Europe, the Americas and Australasia, with an eclectic mixture of both traditional and modern verse, as well as the more abstract and esoteric, and with many of the contributions reflecting the diverse backgrounds and cultures of the writers, *LOVE* is being praised worldwide for its diversity and mix of poets, writers and styles.

Paperback £9.99 (GBP). ISBN: 978-1532701726
Kindle £3.99 (GBP). ASIN: B01HWDINB0

LONELY - A Collection of Poetry and Prose on Loneliness and Being Alone

The FIRST in the Collections of Poetry and Prose book series.

Featuring 118 contributions from 57 writers in 26 countries, with many of the contributions reflecting the diverse backgrounds and cultures of the writers, and all writing in their own unique style, *LONELY - A Collection of Poetry and Prose on Loneliness and Being Alone*, is an extraordinary, unique and eclectic mixture of both traditional and modern verse, and short prose, from writers around the world.

Focusing on just about every aspect of loneliness and being alone, and covering topics as diverse as old age, bereavement, abandonment, divorce, entrapment, unrequited love, depression, trauma, failure and addiction, as well as the more abstract and esoteric, *LONELY* has been acclaimed worldwide for its diversity and mix of writers and styles.

Paperback £9.99 (GBP). ISBN: 978-1523912780
Kindle £3.99 (GBP). ASIN: B01DQLHF70

THE EMPATH - The magazine for Highly Sensitive People

The Empath is probably the only magazines in the world dedicated exclusively to Highly Sensitive People.

In every issue we plan to feature lots and lots of very interesting and informative articles and regular columns from writers, researchers, therapists and empaths around the world about life and living as a Highly Sensitive Person.

The Empath will be published quarterly.

For full details go to:

www.The-Empath.com

www.CollectionsofPoetryandProse.com

www.ingramcontent.com/pod-product-compliance
Lightning Source LLC
Chambersburg PA
CBHW071351280526
45787CB00001B/285